T0357409

School Dinner Heaven

Nostalgic Recipes That Take You Back

Harper
North

WHEN USING KITCHEN APPLIANCES PLEASE ALWAYS
FOLLOW THE MANUFACTURER'S INSTRUCTIONS

HarperNorth
Windmill Green
24 Mount Street
Manchester M2 3NX

A division of
HarperCollins*Publishers*
1 London Bridge Street
London SE1 9GF

www.harpercollins.co.uk

HarperCollins*Publishers*
Macken House
39/40 Mayor Street Upper
Dublin 1
D01 C9W8

First published by HarperNorth in 2024

1 3 5 7 9 10 8 6 4 2

A catalogue record for this book
is available from the British Library

HB ISBN: 978-0-00-871085-9

Printed and bound in Latvia

This book contains FSC™ certified paper and other controlled
sources to ensure responsible forest management.

For more information visit: www.harpercollins.co.uk/green

Contents

Welcome to School Dinner Heaven!

As you read through these pages, you'll find a whole host of recipes that take you back to your school days while also offering a touch of modern flair, alternative cooking suggestions and handy, helpful tips for getting your dinners and lunches ready for school . . . or (sigh) work.

Almost every dish in this book can be served with a big portion of chips, a generous lashing of custard or an untrustworthy amount of gravy to get those nostalgia-laden taste buds excited!

So, get ready to don your apron, embrace your inner dinner lady, and whip up some canteen classics in your own kitchen that hark back to the good old days. Who knew that making **Sprinkle Cake**, **Corn Flake Tart**, **Veggie Burgers** or **Chicken, Leek and Mushroom Pie**, and so much more could be this therapeutic?

Whether you're a seasoned chef or a kitchen novice, these recipes have been designed to be fun, accessible and easy to achieve.

Don't worry, we've left out the 'mystery meat' pie so that you can enjoy the very best dishes from your school days. (Minus the teenage angst!)

General Notes:

- Fruits and Vegetables: Unless otherwise specified, assume all fruits and vegetables are medium-sized.

- Herbs: Use fresh herbs unless dried herbs are explicitly called for in the recipe.

- Eggs: Use free-range eggs.

- Milk: Use whole milk unless a different type is specified.

Store Cupboard Essentials

The ingredients listed below and illustrated on the next page are what you should aim to have in the kitchen to recreate these canteen classics.

Dairy

- butter (unsalted)
- milk (whole or semi-skimmed milk can be used for the majority of these recipes)
- eggs (medium-sized and free-range)
- pastry (ready-made puff and shortcrust pastry is fine to use)

Herbs and Spices

- herbs and spices: salt, pepper, thyme, rosemary, parsley, chilli, paprika, cumin, coriander, garam masala, ginger, cinnamon, nutmeg, bay leaf, chilli flakes, cayenne pepper, basil

Sauces and Condiments

- honey
- jam
- mustard (multiple varieties)
- soy sauce (as stated)
- tomato purée
- Worcestershire sauce

Tins and Jars

- baked beans
- chopped tomatoes
- tinned tuna

Baking

- bicarbonate of soda
- chocolate (dark, milk, white)
- cocoa powder
- desiccated coconut
- digestive biscuits
- flour (self-raising, plain, cornflour)
- pink food colouring
- sprinkles
- sugar (caster, demerara)
- vanilla extract/essence

Kitchen Cupboard

- bread
- corn flakes
- dried noodles
- golden syrup
- oil (olive oil, vegetable)
- puffed rice
- rice
- stock cubes (chicken, lamb, beef)
- suet
- pasta

Break-Time
Bites

Recipes

Sausage Rolls

A timeless classic that is easy to make and perfect for any occasion, whether served warm or cold!

Makes 8 rolls

Preheat oven to 200°C/180°C fan/400°F/gas mark 6

Ingredients

- 1 x 320g packet of ready-made puff pastry
- 450g sausage meat or sausages with skins removed
- 1 beaten egg

Method

1. Roll out the pastry to roughly a 35cm x 30cm rectangle on a lightly floured work surface, trimming any uneven bits so that you have a neat edge. Cut the pastry lengthways in half so that you have two evenly shaped strips of pastry.

2. Add the sausage meat to a large bowl and stir through three tablespoons of cold water before mixing thoroughly. Once combined, remove the sausage meat and divide it into two long, skinless sausages that are roughly the same length as the pastry.

3. Pop each portion of sausage meat into the middle of a pastry strip, leaving enough pastry on either side of the meat. Brush each edge of pastry with the egg and fold one flap over the sausage before rolling it onto the other side and encasing the meat. Gently press any overlapping pastry together with the back of a fork for that classic crimped look.

4. Cut the sausage rolls into 1-inch lengths before placing onto a lined

baking tray and transferring to the fridge for 30 minutes.

5. When you are ready to cook your sausage rolls, brush them with any remaining egg and bake in the oven for 30–35 minutes or until the pastry is a deep golden brown colour.

6. After the sausage rolls are cooked, transfer them to a wire rack and allow to cool for at least 10 minutes before scoffing them all.

Sausages are often easier to find in the supermarket and many of them are pre-spiced, such as Cumberland, or have added ingredients like leek, caramelised onion or apple, which give these sausage rolls an added boost of flavour.

Spread a nice dollop of some good chutney down the centre of the pastry before adding the sausage meat and sprinkling the tops of the sausage rolls with ½ teaspoon of crushed fennel seeds and some rock salt for a more grown-up version of the break-time favourite.

Posh Cheese on Toast

It's not that posh but it's also not your run of the mill, sad-looking cheese on toast from the canteen window – this is brilliant served with any of the soups on pages 20-24.

Serves 2

Ingredients

- 300ml milk
- 50g butter
- 50g plain flour
- 200g mature Cheddar cheese, grated
- 1 tbsp Worcestershire sauce
- 1 tsp English mustard
- ¼ tsp cayenne pepper
- salt and black pepper to taste
- 4 slices of thick bread (white, brown or granary)

Method

1. Make a white sauce using the quantities above, the sauce needs to be a thicker consistency than what you use for a lasagne. (Refer to the method on page 49.)

2. Remove the pan from the heat. Add the rest of the ingredients and stir to combine.

3. Toast the bread lightly under the grill on both sides. Evenly spread the cheese mixture onto one side of the toasted bread.

4. Pop it back under the grill for approx. 2 minutes until the cheese melts and has started to brown a little and bubble. Serve immediately.

Alternative method

1. Put the cheese, Worcestershire sauce and mustard into a bowl and gradually add some milk until the mixture has come together in

a tight spreadable consistency.

2. Toast the bread on one side only and then on the uncooked side spread on the cheese mixture.

3. Pop it back under the grill again for approx. 2 minutes until the cheese melts and has started to brown a little and bubble, serve immediately.

You can use a variety of cheese, such as mature Cheddar with some Gruyère, Edam or Emmental

A dash of brandy or ale can be added to the sauce for a more grown-up taste

Any leftover sauce can be used for other recipes, like Mac and Cheese (page 55) or Lasagne (page 51)

37

40

48

52

Sandwich Fillings

For the days when you didn't fancy anything from the hot section at the canteen or were having one of your parents' homemade sandwiches (including your dad's handprint or an extra treat from mum), there is a list of sandwich fillings across the next couple of pages that can be quickly rustled up using a range of everyday or leftover items from other recipes in School Dinner Heaven.

Makes enough for 1–2 sandwiches

Ingredients

- Bread, wrap or roll of your choice
- 2–3 tbsp of your chosen filling (below)

Method

BBQ Chicken – add a handful (about 100g) of cooked, shredded chicken, 1 tablespoon of sweetcorn and 2 tablespoons of your favourite shop-bought BBQ sauce to a bowl and mix well.

Coronation Chicken – add a handful (about 100g) of cooked, shredded chicken, 1 tablespoon of mayonnaise, 1 teaspoon of mango chutney, and 1 teaspoon of curry powder to a bowl and mix well. You can add a tablespoon of sultanas and ½ tablespoon of flaked almonds for extra texture and sweetness. Season with salt and pepper to taste.

Chicken and Sweetcorn – add a handful (about 100g) of cooked, shredded chicken, 2 tablespoons of drained canned sweetcorn, and 1 tablespoon of mayonnaise to a bowl and mix well. Season with salt and pepper to taste.

Tuna Mayonnaise – add 1 x 145g tin of tuna and between 1–1½ tablespoons of mayonnaise to a bowl with some seasoning and mix well for that classic, comforting filling. Jazz up your tuna mayo by adding ½ tablespoon of capers with some freshly cut chives and dill, sliced spring onion and black pepper.

Egg Mayonnaise – add 2–3 mashed hard-boiled eggs, 2 tablespoons of mayonnaise and 1 teaspoon of Dijon mustard to a bowl and mix well. Season with a pinch of paprika, salt and pepper to taste. (Freshly chopped chives and spring onions also work well with this and it's a great filling for the jacket potatoes on page 27.)

Ham Salad – spread a little butter (mayonnaise or Dijon mustard) on both slices of bread before layering up with 1–2 slices of lettuce, 1 tomato (sliced and lightly salted), ¼ cucumber (sliced) and ½ red onion (sliced) before topping with 1–2 slices of cooked ham.

Cheese and Tomato – add a handful (about 50g) of grated cheese, 1–2 diced tomatoes, and 1 tablespoon of mayonnaise to a bowl and mix well. Season with salt and pepper to taste.

Two Toasties

Classic munch for an extra boost of energy after playing hide-and-seek or kicking a ball around! Each recipe makes one toastie and they can be cooked in a toastie maker but as it's not 1974 anymore, I've included a super-easy way using a frying pan.

Each recipe makes enough for 1 toastie

Ham and Cheese

Ingredients

- 2 slices of bread (your choice)
- 2 slices of ham
- 25g Cheddar cheese, grated or sliced
- 1–2 tsp butter

Cheese and Mushroom Toastie

Ingredients (as above, plus)

Method

- 125g mushrooms, sliced and cooked in ½ tbsp olive oil
- salt and pepper

1. Butter one side of each slice of bread.

2. Place one slice of bread, buttered side down, into a frying pan on a medium heat before adding half the cheese, followed by the ham or cooked mushrooms, then the remaining cheese, before topping with the other piece of bread, buttered side up.

3. Cook for 3–4 minutes on each side until golden brown and crispy. Remove from the pan, cut in half and enjoy hot.

Hedgehog Rolls

An old-school dish from your food tech lessons that makes soft, scrumptious breads that are perfect for dipping into soup or devouring while they're still warm. Careful of the spikes!

Makes 8 rolls

Preheat oven to 220°C/200°C fan/425°F/gas mark 6

Ingredients

- 450g strong white bread flour
- 2 tsp salt
- 1 tsp caster sugar
- 7g fast-action dried yeast
- 50g butter
- 250ml milk
- 1 egg
- sultanas, raisins or pumpkin seeds

Method

1. Add the dry ingredients to one bowl, ensuring that the sugar, salt and yeast are on different sides of the bowl.

2. In a separate microwave-safe bowl, add the milk and butter before placing in the microwave and heating for 1–2 minutes. The butter should be almost melted and the milk should be warm, not hot.

3. Pour the butter and milk mixture into the bowl with the dry ingredients and combine until you form a dough. Once you have a rough ball of dough, add the egg and beat this together.

4. After you have formed the dough, remove it from the bowl and knead it for 5–10 minutes until you have smooth and elastic dough. Place the dough into a lightly oiled bowl and cover with cling film,

leaving it for an hour or until it has doubled in size.

5. When the dough has doubled in size, tip this out onto a lightly floured work surface and gently knock out the air. Divide the dough into 8 pieces and roll each piece of dough into a ball, tucking the sides underneath so that you have a smooth top.

6. After you've made balls, you will need to shape them into hedgehogs, which can be achieved by gently pulling one side of the ball so that it is in the shape of a snout. Take each hedgehog in your hands and use scissors to snip the tops to give the effect of spines. Beginning with a row just behind the 'head' of each hedgehog, work your way backwards to create hedgehog spikes. (Ensure that your snips are large and deep enough so that don't fall back into the dough when baking.)

7. Just before you place the rolls onto the prepared baking tray, add two sultanas or raisins for eyes. Repeat this step with all the rolls, making sure that you leave enough room between each roll to accommodate their second prove. Cover the rolls with cling film and leave them to rise again for around 30 minutes.

8. After the rolls have proved again, place them into the oven and bake for 10-15 minutes or until golden brown. You will know that they're ready when you hear a hollow sound after tapping each roll underneath.

Tomato Soup

An easy-to-make, comforting soup that is reminiscent of your favourite fluorescent-coloured soup from your youth – this is great for a midweek lunch and perfect for dipping into with a hedgehog roll (page 18) or a piece of cheese on toast (page 11).

Serves 2

Preheat oven to 200°C/180°C fan/400°F/gas mark 6

Ingredients

- 6 large tomatoes, cut into eighths
- 1 x 330g pack of cherry tomatoes, cut into halves
- 2 springs onion, cut into quarters
- 4–5 garlic cloves
- 2 tbsp olive oil
- 1 tbsp balsamic vinegar
- 1 tbsp tomato purée

Method

1. Add the tomatoes, spring onions and garlic along with 1 tablespoon of the olive oil and the balsamic vinegar to a baking tray. Bake in the oven for 30–35 minutes or until the tomatoes juices have started to release.

2. Remove the garlic cloves and pour the cooking juices into a jug, reserving for later.

3. Drizzle the remaining olive oil over the tomatoes and add the tomato purée to the tray, mix well and bake for an additional 15 minutes.

4. Remove the tray from the oven. The tomatoes should be sticky

and jammy now. Pour the gooey contents of the tray into a bowl or blender large enough to accommodate the cooked tomatoes and onions (careful, the juices will be hot), and add the reserved cooking juices and sweet garlic (skins removed).

5. Cover the mixture with boiling water so that it just covers the vegetables and blend until smooth.

6. Serve hot with bread and try not to eat it too quickly!

TIPS

Instead of boiling water, use chicken or vegetable stock to top up the liquid. Alternatively, if you've any leftover chopped/plum tinned tomatoes, add these to the mixture before blending to your desired consistency

Adjust the amount of garlic to suit your taste. (No one pays attention anyway!)

Add a red chilli for the same amount of time as the garlic to add a bit more heat. If you'd like less, remove the seeds before adding this to the tray

Leek and Potato Soup

*A classic, creamy soup that is both comforting
and easy to prepare.*

Serves 2

Ingredients

- 25g butter
- 1 medium leek, sliced
- 1 medium potato,
  peeled and diced

- 500ml vegetable stock
- 100ml milk
- salt and pepper

Method

1. Melt the butter in a large saucepan over medium heat.

2. Add the sliced leek and cook for about 5 minutes, until softened.

3. Add the diced potato and cook for another 2 minutes, stirring
   occasionally.

4. Pour in the vegetable stock and bring to a boil.

5. Reduce the heat and simmer for 15–20 minutes,
   until the potatoes are tender.

6. Blend the soup until
   smooth, stir in the milk
   and season with salt
   and pepper to taste.

7. Heat gently until the
   soup is hot, then serve.

Carrot and Coriander Soup

A vibrant and fragrant soup that combines the sweetness of carrots with the freshness of coriander.

Serves 2

Ingredients

- 1 tbsp vegetable oil
- 1 onion, chopped
- 3 medium carrots, peeled and sliced
- 500ml vegetable stock
- small bunch of fresh coriander, chopped
- salt and pepper

Method

1. Heat the vegetable oil in a large saucepan over medium heat.

2. Add the chopped onion and cook for about 5 minutes, until softened.

3. Add the sliced carrots and cook for another 5 minutes, stirring occasionally.

4. Pour in the vegetable stock and bring to a boil.

5. Reduce the heat and simmer for 15-20 minutes, until the carrots are tender.

6. Use a stick blender to blend the soup until smooth.

7. Stir in the chopped coriander and season with salt and pepper to taste.

8. Heat gently until the soup is hot, then serve.

Vegetable Soup

A hearty and wholesome soup packed with a variety of vegetables.

Serves 2

Ingredients

- 1 tbsp olive oil
- 1 onion, chopped
- 1 clove garlic, crushed
- 1 carrot, peeled and diced
- 1 potato, peeled and diced
- 1 courgette, diced
- 500ml vegetable stock
- 200g tinned chopped tomatoes
- 1 tsp dried mixed herbs
- salt and pepper to taste

Method

1. Heat the olive oil in a large saucepan over medium heat.

2. Add the chopped onion and crushed garlic and cook for about 5 minutes, until softened.

3. Add the diced carrot, potato, and courgette, and cook for another 5 minutes, stirring occasionally.

4. Pour in the vegetable stock and add the chopped tomatoes.

5. Stir in the dried mixed herbs and bring to a boil.

6. Reduce the heat and simmer for 20–25 minutes, until all the vegetables are tender.

7. Season with salt and pepper to taste.

8. Heat gently until the soup is hot, then serve.

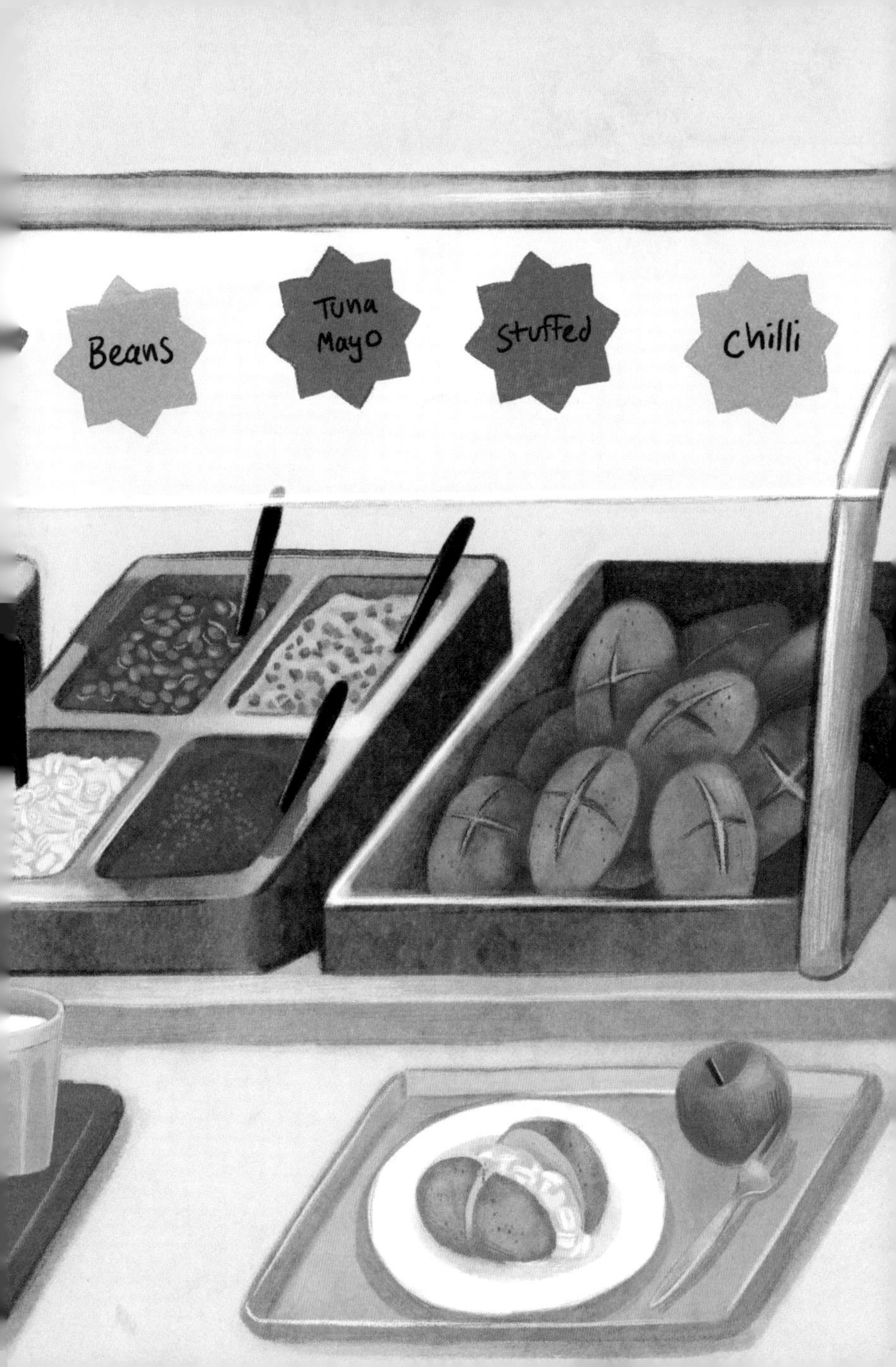
Beans
Tuna Mayo
Stuffed
Chilli

Jacket Potatoes

A regular in the school canteen, the humble jacket potato can be transformed into a delicious midweek lunch or dinner, whether they're loaded with tasty fillings or served with a slab of butter as a side dish, they're quick, easy and incredibly tasty with lots of butter!

Serves 4

Preheat oven to 200°C/180°C fan/400°F/gas mark 6

Ingredients

- 4 medium to large potatoes (good potatoes to use are Maris Piper)
- ½–1 tbsp olive oil
- table salt

Method

1. Wash your potatoes and pat with a piece of paper towel to make sure they are completely dry. Use a fork to gently prick the skin of each potato all over.

2. Rub the skin with the olive oil, you don't need too much, then sprinkle liberally with salt.

3. Place the potatoes on a suitable baking tray and bake for approx. 1–1½ hours, check them after about an hour, the skin should be crispy and the insides pillowy and soft.

Alternatively, you can cook your potatoes by using the below methods:

- If time is short, use your microwave to cook the potatoes. For this quantity and wattage of 900, the potatoes will need to be cooked for approx. 20 minutes turning after 10 minutes.

(You won't get crispy skins with this method but it's a good workaround if you are looking for a quick, comforting meal with lots of butter.)

- Part-cook the potatoes in the microwave for 15 minutes before transferring to the oven and cooking for 40-45 minutes.

- Prepare in the microwave and then transfer to an air fryer and cook for 10 minutes.

Stuffed Jackets

This takes a little bit longer but is well worth the extra time! Once the potatoes are out of the oven, let them cool enough so that you can handle them. Cut the potatoes in half lengthways and carefully scoop out the potato into a bowl, reserve the skins! Mash the potatoes with a little butter and milk, and some grated cheese before refilling the skins with the mashed potato mixture. Sprinkle some more cheese on top and place under a medium–high grill until the cheese has melted and is golden brown on top. You can bulk out these potatoes by adding cooked bacon, peas or any leftover cooked vegetables to the potato mix.

Fillings

Beans and Cheese – gently heat 1 x 415g tin of baked beans with a tablespoon of butter and a few dashes of Worcestershire sauce on a low–medium heat until steaming but not bubbling. Once cooked, slit your potatoes open, add a small handful of grated Cheddar cheese to each potato and divide the beans equally between them. Top with more Cheddar cheese for extra deliciousness.

Soured Cream and Chives – combine 1 x 150ml tub of soured cream with 2–3 tablespoons of freshly chopped chives, a tablespoon of mayonnaise and ½ clove of finely diced garlic before piling on top of your potato.

Coronation Chicken – see page 15 for recipe.
Tuna Mayonnaise – see page 16 for recipe.
Chilli Con Carne – see page 75 for recipe.
Bolognese – see page 47 for recipe.

Canteen
Classics

Recipes

Sausage and Mash

A beloved school canteen classic, sausage and mash is the ultimate comfort food that brings back memories of warm, hearty lunches.

Serves 4

Ingredients

- 500g potatoes, Maris Piper
- 8 sausages of your choice, (2 per person)
- milk and butter, to taste
- 1 portion of gravy (see page 42)

Method

1. Peel the potatoes and cut into quarters, add to a pan of cold water and gently bring to the boil, then simmer until the potatoes are just soft on the inside. Remove from the heat and drain.

2. Leave the potatoes in the pan with the lid slightly covering it, which will enable the potatoes to steam a little and help when mashing.

3. Whilst the potatoes are cooking add your sausages to the grill on a medium–high setting.

4. Place the sausages on the rack and grill on one side until light brown, turn and brown the other side, continue until all sides are brown, taking care not to overcook or burn the sausages. This should take around 20 minutes. Alternatively, you can fry the sausages by adding them to a preheated frying pan, lightly rubbed with some oil to prevent them from sticking. Fry them over a low–medium heat and continue turning them until they are golden brown.

5. When the sausages are ready, transfer to a warm plate and cover to keep them warm.

6. Mash the potatoes, add some milk and butter making sure that the potatoes are holding their own and are not too watery, allow to cool slightly. (You can follow the method from the shepherd's pie recipe on page 83.)

7. Heat your gravy just before serving the sausages on a warmed plate with a dollop of mashed potato (feel free to use an ice-cream scoop to get that classic canteen feel).

Serve with baked beans, peas or broccoli

You can cook your sausages in an air fryer to speed up the cooking process. Please check your appliance instructions

Add some caramelised onion chutney to your gravy for a sweeter kick

Use vegetarian/vegan sausages to make this a vegetarian/vegan product replacement for the sausages, replace the milk and butter with plant-based products

Ham, Egg and Chips

*A British classic that has been served to generations –
ham, egg, and chips is a simple yet utterly satisfying dish
that uses up a host of store cupboard ingredients.*

Serves 4

Preheat oven to 200°C/180°C fan/400°F/gas mark 6

Ingredients

- 4 large potatoes, peeled and cut into ½-inch thick chips
- vegetable oil for frying
- 8 slices cold cooked ham

- 4 large eggs
- 1 tbsp olive oil
- salt and pepper to taste

Method

Chips

For each of the methods detailed below, make sure that you rinse the cut potato chips in cold water until the water runs clear to remove excess starch before thoroughly patting dry with paper towels.

Frying

Heat 2–3 inches of vegetable oil in a deep pot or Dutch oven to 325°F (165°C). Fry the potato chips in batches for 5–7 minutes until lightly golden. Drain on a wire rack or paper towel-lined plate and season with salt.

Oven

Heat the oven to 200°C/180°C fan/400°F/gas mark 6, put the dried chips into a plastic bag with 1½ tablespoons olive oil and 1 teaspoon sea salt and shake to coat. Place the coated chips evenly spaced onto non-stick baking trays and cook in the oven for approx. 35–40 minutes, turning occasionally until brown and crispy but soft inside.

Air Fryer

Put the dried chips into a plastic bag with 1½ tablespoons olive oil and 1 teaspoon sea salt and shake to coat. Depending on your air fryer, empty the chips from the bag into the drawer/drawers and cook in batches to avoid any overcrowding. Cook on Air Fry setting at 200°C/400°F and air fry for 15–20 minutes, shaking the basket occasionally to ensure even cooking. Cook until golden brown and crispy. Keep warm in the oven until ready to serve.

Ham and Eggs

1. Place the cold sliced ham on a plate and cover loosely with foil to warm up in the oven for 5 minutes.

2. While your ham is warming through in the oven, add the oil to a medium-sized frying pan over a medium heat and fry your eggs until the whites are cooked and the yolks are still runny. This will take 3–4 minutes (longer if you prefer your yolks to be more set).

3. Once the eggs are cooked, remove the ham from the oven and add one egg to each plate with a handful of chips.

4. Season with salt and pepper and serve.

TIPS

Chips can be made in advance and reheated in the oven at 200°C/180°C fan/400°F/gas mark 6 for 30–40 minutes until hot and crispy

Alternative seasonings: paprika, garlic salt, mild chilli powder, black pepper

Instead of frying your eggs, you can poach them in 3–4 inches of just simmering water with 1–2 tbsp of white wine vinegar for 3–4 minutes for perfectly poached eggs with a runny yolk

Roast Chicken

Simple, satisfying and a perfect Sunday dish – just like the dinner ladies do, any leftover chicken can be used in other recipes from this book, like the sandwich fillings on pages 15–16 or to bulk out the fajitas on page 71.

Preheat oven to 190°C/170°C fan/375°F/gas mark 5

Ingredients

- 1 whole chicken (approx. 1.5–2kg)
- 1 lemon, quartered
- 1 onion, quartered
- 2 carrots, peeled and cut into chunks
- 2 stalks celery, cut into chunks
- 2 sprigs thyme
- 2 sprigs rosemary
- 2 tbsp butter, softened
- 250ml chicken stock or water
- 2 tbsp plain flour
- 2 tbsp cold water
- gravy browning
- salt and pepper, to taste

Method

1. Prepare the chicken, season the cavity with salt and black pepper, add the lemon and onion quarters and a few carrots and celery chunks, add one sprig each of the thyme and rosemary. Then tie the chicken legs together with kitchen string and tuck the wing tips under the body.

2. Rub the softened butter all over the outside of the chicken and season with salt and pepper.

3. Place the remaining vegetables and herbs in the roasting tin and sit the chicken on top. Roast the chicken for approx. 1 hour 15 minutes to 1 hour 30 minutes, baste the chicken with the juices from the

roasting tin occasionally. The chicken is ready once the juices run clear and when the thickest part of the thigh is pierced with a fork. Remove from the oven and transfer to another plate and allow it to rest for about 10–15 minutes while you make the gravy (recipe on page 42).

4. Skim any of the excess fat from the juices in the roasting tin, and over medium heat whisk in the flour until it is combined. For a rich colour add a few drops of gravy browning to the tin, taste and add any seasoning if necessary. Cook for about 2 to 3 minutes whisking constantly. Add more water if required. If you prefer, you can transfer the juices to a saucepan and cook in the same way.

5. Carve the chicken and serve hot with roasted vegetables, roast potatoes, stuffing, Yorkshire puddings and gravy.

TIPS

For extra flavour, rub the chicken with a mixture of butter, herbs and lemon zest before roasting

Can be cooked in the air fryer, refer to your appliance cooking times

Use the carcass and boil it in a large pot to make chicken stock. Simply add the carcass alongside some chopped carrots, celery and onion before covering with water. Bring to the boil and after 45–60 minutes, sieve the juices into a pan, if using straightaway, or an airtight container to use when required. The juices can be frozen in freezer bags and used within 3 months. This adds a lot of flavour to the soups on pages 20–24, but does mean that they are not vegetarian-friendly soups!

Roast Beef

Perfectly cooked roast beef (not a regular occurrence in schools) is absolutely fantastic served with lashings of gravy, cauliflower cheese, roast potatoes, Yorkshire pudding, a dollop of English mustard or whatever else takes your fancy. Pass me the horseradish!

Serves 4-6

Preheat oven to 220°C/200°C fan/425°F/gas mark 7

Ingredients

- approx. 875g boneless rib of beef
- ½ tbsp olive oil, plus ½ tbsp for searing the beef
- 1 tsp mustard powder
- black pepper, to taste

Method

1. Allow the beef to stand at room temperature for a good half an hour.

2. Rub the beef with the oil, mustard powder and some pepper. Heat a large frying pan until it is very hot and the oil is shimmering. Once the oil is up to temperature, add the beef to the pan and sear it, moving it around to seal it all over with a browned tinge, which should take a few minutes.

3. After the beef has browned all over, remove it from the pan and place it into a roasting tin before adding it to the preheated oven. Cook for 15 minutes and then turn the temperature down to 180°C/ 160°C fan/350°F/gas mark 4 and cook for an additional 60 minutes for rare to medium (cooking times are detailed on the next page).

4. Remove the beef from the oven, reserve any meat juices to make

a gravy (page 42) and place the beef on a plate to rest for half the cooking time.

5. Once rested, carve the beef and serve with a host of your favourite side dishes, such as cauliflower cheese (page 41), Yorkshire pudding (page 43) and roast potatoes (page 44).

TIPS

20 minutes per 500g plus 20 minutes for rare

25 minutes per 500g plus 20 minutes for medium

30 minutes per 500g plus 20 minutes for well done

Cauliflower Cheese

Creamy and cheesy goodness – another amazing side dish to serve alongside a roast dinner for a touch of extra indulgence.

Serves 4-6

Preheat oven to 200°C/180°C fan/400°F/gas mark 6

Ingredients

- 1 medium or ½ a large cauliflower, cut into florets
- ½ tbsp olive oil
- 250ml milk
- 15g cornflour
- ½ tsp mustard powder

- ½ tsp crushed garlic
- 65g mature Cheddar cheese
- 35g Parmesan cheese
- 15g Red Leicester cheese
- 2 tbsp breadcrumbs
- salt and pepper, to taste

Method

1. Place the cauliflower in an ovenproof dish, drizzle over the oil season with salt and pepper. Place in the preheated oven for approx. 10 minutes until it has started to soften slightly and is lightly charred on top.

2. In a non-stick saucepan, gently heat the milk until it is just warm. Mix the cornflour with some cold water and slowly add this to the warmed milk whisking all the time, add the mustard powder and garlic and continue whisking until the mixture thickens. Remove from the heat and add 50g of the mature Cheddar and all the Parmesan, then continue cooking on a low heat for approx. five minutes until everything is mixed and thickened.

3. Pour the sauce over the cauliflower evenly, sprinkle over the remaining cheeses and breadcrumbs. Bake in the oven for approx. 15–20 minutes until the cauliflower is soft and the top is golden brown.

Gravy

Glistening, thick, tasty gravy? Yes, please. This is a
fantastic accompaniment to many of the dishes in
this book and, well, let's be honest – everything
tastes better with gravy!

Makes 4-6 portions

Ingredients

- leftover meat juices, see Roast Chicken (page 37) and Roast Beef (page 39)
- 1–2 tsp cornflour, mixed with small amount of water (about 1 tsp)
- dash of gravy browning
- salt and pepper, to taste

Method

1. Put all the meat juices into a small pan and add approx. 250–280ml of hot water. If you are cooking any vegetables as a side dish to accompany a main meal, you can use some of that water to add additional flavour to the gravy.

2. Place the pan over a low heat and slowly add the cornflour slurry, mixing all the time until it starts to thicken, add more cornflour mixed with water if you desire a thicker consistency.

3. Once the gravy has thickened, add a dash or two of gravy browning before seasoning with salt and pepper. Continue to cook the gravy for a few minutes until you are ready to serve.

 You can add a little bit of the Yorkshire pudding batter on the next page to thicken up your gravy

Alternatively, if you have a very small amount of meat juices available use gravy granules and mix accordingly to bulk out the gravy

Yorkshire Pudding

Yorkshire pudding is the perfect accompaniment to a roast, soaking up all of that delicious gravy.

Makes 12 portions

Preheat oven to 230°C/210°C fan/460°F/gas mark 8

Ingredients

- 5 medium eggs
- 200ml milk
- 100ml water

- 240g plain flour
- salt and pepper
- vegetable oil

Method

1. In a large mixing bowl or mixer add the eggs, milk, water, flour and seasoning before mixing for approx. 5 minutes or until you have a light bubbly mixture. There should be no lumps.

2. Pour into a suitable jug and leave in the fridge for at least 2 hours or for best results overnight. Stir before using.

3. In your Yorkshire pudding trays add between ½ and 1 teaspoon of oil to each section and then place your tray back into the hot oven until the oil is ready.

4. Once your oil is ready (you will know it is done when the oil is smoking or when a small amount of the mixture begins to sizzle when dropped directly into the fat), fill each hole to approx. two-thirds and then carefully transfer the tray back to the oven. Bake for 20–25 minutes and avoid opening the oven door while cooking as your puddings will collapse if opened too early.

5. Remove from the oven and let your Yorkshire puddings cool before removing them from the tins.

Roast Potatoes

Crispy, crunchy, soft in the middle – a roast dinner just isn't the same without a pile of these.

Serves 4

Preheat oven to 200°C/180°C fan/400°F/gas mark 6

Ingredients

- 800g potatoes
  (Maris Piper are great)

- 2 tbsp vegetable oil
  or goose fat

Method

1. Peel and cut the potatoes in half before adding to a large pan of cold water on a medium–high heat. Bring this pan to the boil then turn the heat down to medium and cook for about 5–7 minutes until the edges are just going soft but the centres still have some resistance when pierced with a knife.

2. While the potatoes are cooking heat the oil or goose fat in a large roasting tin until it is very hot and shimmering.

3. Once the potatoes are done, remove them from the heat and drain them immediately. Leave them in the pan with the lid on for 10–15 minutes to steam.

4. When you are ready to roast the potatoes, gently shake the covered pan to give the potatoes a rough edge, which will turn crispy when roasted. Carefully transfer the potatoes to the hot roasting tin, turn them over in the oil to coat them and before roasting in the oven, turning occasionally, for 45–50 minutes.

5. Remove from the oven and transfer to a warmed dish ready to serve.

Chicken Tikka Masala

While this is not a traditional version of the Indian dish, which takes anywhere from twelve hours to a day to prepare and cook, it is incredibly flavoursome and often a quicker, healthier and cheaper option than your local takeaway.

Makes 6 - 8 portions

Preheat oven to 180°C/160°C fan/350°F/gas mark 4

Ingredients

- 1kg chicken cut into bite-sized chunks (use boneless, skinless thighs or chicken breasts)
- 2 tbsp olive oil
- 1 large onion, finely chopped
- 3 garlic cloves, finely chopped
- 1 tbsp grated fresh ginger
- 2 tsp garam masala
- 1 tsp ground cumin
- 1 tsp ground coriander
- 1 tsp paprika
- 1 tsp chilli powder
- 1 tsp salt
- 1 x 400g tin chopped tomatoes
- 300ml double cream
- 2 tbsp tomato purée
- 1 tbsp lemon juice

Method

1. Heat the olive oil in a large frying pan or ovenproof dish on a medium heat, add the chicken and cook until it is lightly browned on all sides for about 5–7 minutes. Remove the chicken from the pan.

2. In the same pan, add the onion and cook for 2–3 minutes until softened then add the garlic and ginger and cook for 1 minute, stirring constantly.

3. Stir in the rest of the spices and salt and cook for about 1 minute, stirring constantly.

4. Add the chopped tomatoes, cream, tomato purée and lemon juice, stir and let it simmer for a few minutes and then add the chicken back to the pan.

5. Cover the pan and cook in the preheated oven for 30–40 minutes, or until the chicken is cooked through and the sauce has thickened.

TIPS

Serve with rice or naan

Add some fresh coriander as a garnish before serving

Substitute the cream with Greek yogurt

For an even quicker version, use frozen onions, garlic and ginger and a tikka spice mix or paste

Spaghetti 'Bolognese'

Lovingly referred to as 'spag bol' across the country, its rich, meaty sauce, was the beloved school dinner that made you feel right at home.

Serves 4-6

Ingredients

- 2 tbsp olive oil
- 1 large onion
- 2 carrots
- 2 sticks celery
- 1 garlic clove, chopped (optional)
- 500g minced beef
- 1 beef stock cube

- 1 tbsp tomato purée
- 1 x 500g jar passata
- 250ml water
- 400–600g spaghetti (100g per person)
- handful of fresh basil
- Cheddar cheese, to serve

Method

1. Heat the oil in a large deep frying pan, sauté the onions, carrots, celery and garlic if desired until softened. Remove the vegetables and set aside.

2. In the same pan cook the mince on a medium–high heat until browned, stirring to avoid any burning. Return the vegetables to the mince and stir.

3. Crumble the stock cube over the mince before adding the tomato purèe and cooking out for 1–2 minutes.

4. Add the passata and bring to a gentle simmer, before adding 250ml of water to the pan and increasing the heat. Once the mixture has come to a boil, turn the heat down and simmer on a low–medium heat for 35–40 minutes until the sauce has thickened.

5. As the sauce is nearing the end of its cooking time, boil another pan of water and cook the spaghetti according to package instructions. (You can use more or less pasta depending on how hungry you are but 100g per person is a decent portion.)

6. Dollop a generous helping of the sauce on top of a nest of spaghetti before topping with some freshly chopped basil and a good grating of Cheddar (just don't tell the Italians!)

TIPS

This sauce is brilliant as a jacket potato filling

You can portion this into freezer bags so that you always have a ready-made pasta sauce

To make this a vegetarian-friendly option: add 250g puy lentils instead of the beef, 500ml of vegetable stock instead of the beef stock and 1 tablespoon of either cider or balsamic vinegar.

White Sauce

This is the base sauce to a lot of the recipes in this book (including the lasagne on page 51) – it is easy to make and I have included two versions here that can be used to fit around your day.

Makes approx. 300ml

Ingredients

- 50g butter
- 500ml whole milk

- 30g plain flour
- salt and pepper, to taste

The 'classic' roux method

1. Melt the butter in a non-stick pan over a medium heat, once melted and gently bubbling, add the flour and reduce the heat, stirring continuously and allowing time for the flour to blend with the butter until you have a paste like consistency.

2. Slowly add the milk a bit at a time, stirring continuously until the butter-and-flour paste is well incorporated with each addition of milk. Keep slowly adding a small amount of milk to the pan while stirring until you are left with no more milk. Continue stirring for a few minutes before taking off the heat. You should now have a lump-free sauce.

The all-in-one method (a quick-and-easy version of the previous recipe for when you are short on time).

- Add all the ingredients to a pan over a medium heat and whisk continuously until the sauce begins to thicken. This can take up to 5 minutes.

- Once thickened, continue to cook the sauce through while whisking for another few minutes before taking off the heat.

(This method is a lot quicker than the roux method but some say that you can taste the flour if it is not 'cooked' once it has thickened.)

TIPS

Can be used in recipes in the book, for example:
Lasagne, Fish Pie, Mac and Cheese

Add mustard powder or Worcestershire sauce for flavourings

Lasagne

*A square of oozing, richly layered flavours that uses two
other recipes in this book – White Sauce (see page 49)
and Spaghetti 'Bolognese' (see page 47) – to make
this canteen favourite.*

Serves 6-8

Preheat oven to 180°C/160°C fan/350°F/gas mark 4

Ingredients

For the lasagne

- 1 portion of Bolognese (see page 47)
- or 1 portion of vegetarian Bolognese sauce (see Tips on the recipe page)
- 1 portion (300ml) white sauce (see page 49)
- 2 tsp Dijon mustard
- 100g grated Cheddar cheese
- 1 x 250g packet fresh lasagne pasta sheets (you can freeze any leftover sheets)

For the topping

- 50g Cheddar
- 50g mozzarella
- 25g Parmesan

Method

1. Make the Bolognese and remove from the heat.

2. Make the white sauce. Once the sauce has thickened, add the mustard and cheese to the sauce over a low heat and cook for approx. 5 minutes, stirring continuously until all the cheese has been melted into the sauce. Remove from the heat and set aside.

3. If you are making the Bolognese specifically for this recipe at the same time, follow the instructions then set the pan aside before assembling the lasagne.

4. Once you have all the above elements you can then prepare your lasagne dish. Layer the dish as follows:

   - Put a thin layer (approx. 2–3 tbsp) of the Bolognese sauce in the bottom of the dish.

   - Place a layer (avoiding overlap) of lasagne sheets over the top of the sauce.

   - Then a layer of the white sauce to cover.

   - Finishing with the Bolognese sauce on the top.

   - Repeat until all of your Bolognese and white sauce has gone.

5. Mix the Cheddar and mozzarella together and scatter over the final layer of Bolognese, before topping with the Parmesan.

6. Bake in the oven for 30–35 minutes until golden brown and bubbling.

For a vegetarian option – roast some vegetables such as aubergine, courgettes, onions, peppers, butternut squash, etc., and add these to the sauce before layering in the same way

Freezes well – leave to go completely cold and then cut into required portions – I wrap the ready-made squares of lasagne in baking parchment and then bags. Each portion can be defrosted and heated in the oven at 180°C for approx. 15–20 minutes

Irish Stew

A humble, leave-it-to-cook dish that's brimming with flavour – the ultimate comfort food during the chilly winter months.

Serves 6-8

Preheat oven to 150°C/130°C fan/300°F/gas mark 2

Ingredients

- 1–1.5kg lamb shoulder or neck, diced into 1-inch cubes
- olive oil, for frying
- plain flour, for dusting
- 1 large onion, finely sliced
- 1 large leek, finely sliced
- 2 garlic cloves, crushed and finely chopped
- 2 large carrots, cut into chunks

- fresh thyme and flat leaf parsley, 2 sprigs of each or 1 tsp each of dried herbs
- 1 bay leaf
- 1l beef stock
- 3 large potatoes, cut into quarters
- 8 baby carrots, washed
- 1 tbsp Worcestershire sauce
- salt and pepper, to taste

Method

1. Heat some olive oil in an ovenproof casserole dish. Cut the lamb into cubes and then dust with some flour. When the oil is hot cook the lamb in batches until brown on all sides, remove the first batch and continue to cook until all the lamb is browned and then set aside.

2. Using the same dish add the onions, leeks, and garlic and cook over a medium heat until softened.

3. Add the lamb back to the casserole with the carrots, herbs, bay leaf and stock. Stir to combine everything, bring to a simmer.

4. Cook in the oven with the lid on for approx. 2–2½ hours.

5. Remove from the oven and add the potatoes and baby carrots, return to the oven and cook for a further 30 minutes. Check that the potatoes are cooked and the lamb is tender, if not return to the oven for a further 10 minutes until cooked.

6. Season with salt and pepper, remove the bay leaf and finally, stir in the Worcestershire sauce.

TIPS

Pop the flour, about 1 tablespoon, into a plastic bag
and shake the lamb to cover

Serve with mashed potatoes (use the recipe on page 83) and peas

Slow cooking is also ideal for this recipe, approx. 8 hours depending
on your slow cooker

Mac and Cheese

A cheesy, comforting dish that's guaranteed to fill you up – this recipe is for a classic Mac and Cheese but is a great base recipe to add your own twists too. There are a few tips on the next page to help you get started ...

Serves 4

Ingredients

For the Mac and Cheese

- 1 portion (300ml) white sauce (see page 49)
- 125g Cheddar cheese, grated
- ½ tsp freshly grated nutmeg
- 1 tsp wholegrain mustard
- 350g macaroni

For the topping

- handful of corn flakes
- 50g parmesan, finely grated
- ½ tbsp olive oil

Method

1. Make the white sauce as described on page 49. Once thickened, stir in the Cheddar, nutmeg and wholegrain mustard before returning to the heat and cooking on a low heat for approx. 5 minutes.

2. Fill a large pan with water and bring it to the boil, add a pinch of salt, then add your pasta. Cook the pasta until it is soft enough to bite, approx. 8–10 minutes. Drain the pasta and set aside.

3. Add the cheese sauce to the macaroni and stir it through to coat each macaroni with the cheesy sauce. Add a small dash of pasta water if the sauce has thickened too much. Season with salt and pepper then add to a 30 x 30cm baking dish.

4. Crush the corn flakes into a breadcrumb consistency and scatter over the macaroni cheese before covering with the Parmesan and a drizzle of olive oil.

5. Bake in the oven for 30–35 minutes, turning halfway through to ensure a crispy top. Once cooked, remove and allow to cool for 5 minutes before serving.

Fry up some bacon, chorizo or pancetta to mix through for a meaty mac and cheese

Throw in in some frozen peas, a handful of blanched spinach, some spring onions and stir freshly cut chives through the sauce mix for a veggie-packed version

Use a combination of different cheeses such as Cheddar, mozzarella, blue cheese, Gruyère and Emmental for a more grown-up, sophisticated version

Stale bread can be blitzed in a food processor as an alternative to the corn flake topping

Pepperoni
Sheet-Pan Pizza

A delicious sheet-pan pizza recipe reminiscent of the huge slabs the dinner ladies served up – this uses the same dough recipe as Hedgehog Rolls on page 18. I've used pepperoni as a topping here, but you can put whatever you like on yours!

Serves 4

Ingredients

For the dough

- 450g strong white bread flour
- 2 tsp salt
- 1 tsp caster sugar
- 7g fast-action dried yeast
- 50g butter
- 250ml milk (whole or semi-skimmed)
- 1 egg

For the topping

- 1 x 400g tin chopped tomatoes
- 2 tsp dried oregano, 1 ½ tsp for the sauce and ½ tsp for the top
- 200g shredded mozzarella cheese
- 100g sliced pepperoni
- fresh basil leaves, to serve

Method

1. Add the dry ingredients to one bowl, ensuring that the sugar, salt and yeast are on different sides of the bowl.

2. In a separate microwave-safe bowl, add the milk and butter before

placing in the microwave and heating for 1–2 minutes. The butter should be almost melted and the milk should be warm, not hot.

3. Pour the butter and milk mixture into the bowl with the dry ingredients and combine until you form a dough. Once you have a rough ball of dough, add the egg and beat this together.

4. After you have formed the dough, remove it from the bowl and knead it for 5–10 minutes until you have smooth and elastic dough. Place the dough into a lightly oiled bowl and cover with cling film, leaving it for an hour or until it has doubled in size.

5. Once the dough has doubled in size, gently punch it down to release air bubbles. Transfer the dough to the prepared sheet pan and press it out to cover the pan evenly.

6. Preheat your oven to 220°C/200°C fan/425°F/gas mark 7. Lightly grease a large sheet pan with olive oil.

7. To make a simple pizza sauce, crush the chopped tomatoes with your hands (a great way to get the kids involved!) and add a teaspoon of oregano to the tomatoes. Stir to combine, season and then spread over the top of your pizza, making sure that you leave a border for the crust.

8. Sprinkle the shredded mozzarella cheese over the sauce. Arrange the sliced pepperoni over the cheese. Sprinkle the top with the remaining oregano.

9. Bake for 20–25 minutes, or until the crust is golden brown and the cheese is melted and bubbly.

10. Remove from the oven and let cool for a few minutes before slicing. Garnish with fresh basil leaves if desired. Enjoy your delicious homemade pepperoni sheet-pan pizza!

Vegetable Stir-Fry with Noodles

A delightfully quick and adaptable dish that let's you use up what you have in!

Serves 4

Ingredients

- 2 tbsp vegetable oil
- 1 large onion, sliced
- 1 red pepper, deseeded and sliced
- 1 yellow pepper, deseeded and sliced
- 3 carrots, peeled and sliced thinly lengthways
- 1 courgette, peeled and chopped into chunks
- 1 head of broccoli, florets only
- 250g noodles (dried), to serve

For the sauce

- juice of ½ lemon
- 50ml soy sauce (dark or light)
- 50ml vegetable stock
- 1 tsp chopped garlic
- 1 tsp grated ginger
- 2 tbsp honey
- 1 tbsp sesame oil
- 1 tbsp apple cider vinegar
- 1 tbsp cornflour
- pinch of chilli flakes (optional)

Method

1. Combine all the sauce ingredients together in a bowl or jar and set aside until you are ready to cook.

2. Bring a large pan of water to the boil ready for you to cook your noodles.

3. Heat a large pan or wok with the oil on a medium–high heat, once hot add all the ingredients except the broccoli and courgette, stir-fry for approx. 6–8 minutes. Add the broccoli and courgettes and continue stir-frying for another 4–5 minutes, until everything is cooked but still retains a crunch.

4. Once you have added the broccoli and courgette to the pan, put your noodles into the already-boiling water and cook over a medium heat for approx. 5 minutes or until soft, remove from the heat and drain.

5. While the noodles are cooking, stir the sauce to make sure that the cornflour is thoroughly mixed with the rest of the ingredients and add it a tablespoon at a time to the hot cooked vegetables, stirring all the time until it has thickened. (You will use around half of the sauce for this recipe – the remaining sauce can be stored in the fridge for up to seven days.)

6. Place the cooked noodles in a bowl, top with the vegetables and serve.

Top with some freshly cut red chilli, spring onion and coriander

Fresh noodles can also be used and some don't require pre-cooking. Check the packet for instructions

Other vegetables, such as mangetout, sugar snap peas, mushrooms and shredded cabbage can be substituted depending on what you have in your fridge

Swap out the noodles for cooked rice (day-old rice is usually better for this and soaks up more of the flavour)

Using rice noodles makes this dish suitable for vegetarians. (Changing the noodles and using agave or another alternative for honey, makes this dish vegan-friendly.)

Tuna Pasta Bake

A great dish to make if you've got any leftover white sauce to use up and want to do something with those tins of tuna that you've not used for two years.

Serves 6-8

Preheat oven to 180°C/160°C fan/350°F/gas mark 4

Ingredients

- 500g dried pasta (penne or fusilli)
- 1 portion (300ml) white sauce (see page 49)
- 1 tbsp olive oil
- 250g Cheddar cheese, grated
- 1 tsp dried mixed herbs

- 1 large onion, finely chopped
- 2 garlic cloves, crushed
- 3 x 160g tins tuna in brine, drained
- 100g frozen peas
- 50g breadcrumbs
- salt and pepper, to taste

Method

1. Cook the pasta in a large pan of salted boiling water, usually around 8–10 minutes, so that it retains some of its bite. Once cooked, drain, retaining a small amount of the pasta water (around a cupful) and set aside.

2. Make white sauce. When the sauce has thickened, add in half the grated cheese, season with salt and pepper and add the herbs, stir until the cheese has melted and the sauce is well combined. Set aside to cool slightly while you cook the onions and garlic.

3. Gently heat the oil in a frying pan over medium heat and cook the onions and garlic until softened.

4. In a large mixing bowl, combine the cooked pasta, cheese sauce, drained tuna and frozen peas. Mix well.

5. Transfer the mixture to a large ovenproof dish. Top with the remaining grated cheese and sprinkle with breadcrumbs.

6. Bake in the preheated oven for 25–30 minutes, until the top is golden brown and crispy.

7. Allow to cool for 5 minutes before serving.

TIPS

For an extra-crispy crunch, add some crushed-up corn flakes to the top and dot with butter

Serve with a side of steamed vegetables or a simple green salad

Leftovers can be refrigerated and reheated the next day – 'It tastes even better.' (As us dinner ladies would say!)

Add 200g of chopped tinned tomatoes (around half a standard tin) to the final mix for a cheese and tomato-based sauce

Peas can be substituted with tinned sweetcorn if preferred, or a mix of both

Fish Pie

A creamy, comforting Fish Friday classic that you could smell from down the hallway while sitting in Biology.

Serves 6-8

Preheat oven to 200°C/180°C fan/400°F/gas mark 6

Ingredients

- 1kg potatoes, peeled and cut into chunks
- 300ml milk
- 250ml single cream
- 1 stick celery, finely chopped
- 1 small carrot, peeled and finely chopped
- 1 small leek, white part only, washed and finely chopped
- ½ tsp dried thyme
- 500g mixed white fish, you can use haddock (smoked or plain) cod, pollock and salmon, cut into chunks
- 50g butter
- 50g plain flour
- ½ tbsp wholegrain mustard
- 1 tbsp chopped parsley
- 50g butter (for the sauce)
- 50ml milk (for the sauce)
- 200g prawns
- 50g frozen peas (optional)
- 100g grated mature Cheddar cheese (optional)
- 50g breadcrumbs

Method

1. In a large pan of boiling water, cook the potatoes until they are soft but not falling apart.

2. At the same time, in another medium-sized saucepan over a medium heat, add the milk, cream, celery, leek, carrots and thyme. Bring this mixture to a just-warm temperature before adding all the fish, except for the prawns, and poaching for 10 minutes.

3. After the time is up, turn off the heat on both pans and drain your potatoes. (You can leave these to cool slightly in the pan, ready to be mashed.)

4. Strain the fish-infused milk into a bowl and reserve it so that you can make the sauce from it. Remove the cooked fish from the liquid, break into flakes and set aside in a separate bowl.

5. With the flour and butter quantities on the facing page, make a sauce as described on page 49 with the remaining poaching liquid that has been strained. You will need a fairly thick sauce here, so the remaining milk (150ml) on page 49 should be enough for the sauce if too much of the liquid has evaporated during cooking. If you prefer a looser sauce, add a dash more milk.

6. Once the sauce has thickened, remove the pan from the heat and add the mustard and chopped parsley, seasoning to taste. Add the flaked fish, prawns and frozen peas, stir gently to combine. (Take care not to over-stir here or the fish will become mushy.)

7. Make the mashed potato using the method given on page 83.

8. In shallow ovenproof dish, add the fish and sauce mixture, cover with the mashed potato, followed by a generous sprinkling of cheese (if using) and the breadcrumbs.

9. Bake in a preheated oven for 25–30 minutes until the top is golden brown and the filling is bubbling.

A frozen fish pie mixture can be used, but be sure to defrost it first

Leftovers can be frozen in portions and defrosted overnight in the fridge, reheat in the oven for about 10–15 minutes until hot

Choice of fish used is up to you but a smoked fish, such as haddock, gives an added taste to the dish

Lancashire Hotpot

Just like Betty used to make on Coronation Street – this recipe is full of flavour and can be served with a whole host of sides.

Serves 4-6

Preheat oven to 180°C/160°C fan/350°F/gas mark 4

Ingredients

- 500g lamb shoulder or neck, cut into chunks
- 2 large potatoes, peeled and thinly sliced
- 1 large onion, thinly sliced
- 1 large carrot, peeled and thinly sliced
- ½ tsp dried thyme
- ½ tsp dried rosemary
- 1 bay leaf
- 300ml lamb stock
- 15g butter
- salt and pepper, to taste

Method

1. Prepare all the vegetables and meat and divide them separately in half. Use a large ovenproof dish and layer half of the sliced potatoes, onions, carrots, and lamb. Add the salt, pepper, thyme, rosemary, and bay leaf. Then repeat the layers with the remaining potatoes, onions, carrots, and lamb, finishing with a layer of potatoes on the top. Pour the stock over the top and make sure it is all covered with the liquid, gently push the vegetables and meat a little to get them covered.

2. Cut the butter into cubes and scatter over the top of the potato layer, cover the dish with a lid and bake for 1–1½ hours.

3. Remove the lid and cook for another 15 minutes. For a crispy potato top, increase the temperature to 200°C/180°C fan/400°F/gas mark 6 for the last 15 minutes.

4. Remove the bay leaf before serving.

TIPS

You can use stewing steak as an alternative to the lamb shoulder or neck

· Pickled red cabbage goes well with this dish

You can freeze any leftovers, defrost thoroughly overnight in the fridge and reheat in the oven

Veggie Burgers

These burgers are really easy to make when you're short for time and are loved by carnivores and vegetarians alike.

Serves 4

Ingredients

- 1 x 400g tin chickpeas, drained
- zest and juice of ½ lemon
- 1 tsp ground cumin
- 1 tsp smoked paprika
- small bunch of coriander, chopped
- 1 egg
- 100g breadcrumbs
- 1 red onion (½ diced, ½ sliced thinly into rings)

- 1 tbsp olive oil
- 2 tbsp sweet chilli sauce
- 2 tbsp Greek yogurt
- 4 burger buns (white, brown or wholemeal)
- 1 avocado, sliced
- 1 large tomato, sliced
- ½ cucumber, sliced

Method

1. In a food processor, combine the chickpeas, lemon zest, lemon juice, cumin, paprika, half the coriander, egg, and salt and pepper. Process the mixture until smooth. Transfer to a bowl and mix in 80g of breadcrumbs and the diced red onion. Shape the mixture into four equal-sized burgers, pressing the remaining breadcrumbs onto both sides so that you can crisp the burgers while cooking. Chill for 10-15 minutes.

2. Heat the olive oil in a frying pan over a medium heat. Fry each burger for 4 minutes on each side, until golden brown and heated through.

3. Mix the sweet chilli sauce and yogurt together in a bowl to combine before assembling your burgers.

4. To assemble: slice each bun and layer with slices of avocado and a slice of tomato, the veggie burger, a couple of rings of the red onion and some cucumber slices. Spread some chilli sauce on the other side of the bun and add any remaining chopped coriander.

Roast off any leftover bell peppers in an oven at
180°C / 160°C fan / 350°F / gas mark 4 for 15–20 minutes,
until slightly charred and soft, before adding these as a
topping to your burger

Quiche Lorraine

A dish that people love or loathe – this is great eaten hot or cold and is brilliant for summertime picnics. This pastry also works great with the Cheese and Onion Pie on page 77.

Serves 6-8

Preheat oven to 180°C/160°C fan/350°F/gas mark 4

Ingredients

For the pastry

- 125g plain flour
- 60g butter
- cold water, approx. 1 tbsp

For the filling

- 1 tbsp olive oil
- 1 onion, chopped
- 180g bacon, chopped
- 2 eggs
- 250ml milk
- 125g mature Cheddar cheese, grated

Method

1. Make the pastry first, put the flour into a bowl and rub in the butter to create fine breadcrumbs, slowly mix the cold water in either with your hands or a knife until it comes together, make sure it is not too sticky, if it is just add a little more flour. Make it into a ball and wrap in some cling film and pop it in the fridge so that it can chill for about 30–40 minutes.

2. Take the pastry out of the fridge and dust your work surface with a little flour, roll out and line a 20cm pie dish. Blind bake in the oven for 10–12 minutes using ceramic baking beans. Take out

of the oven and leave to cool in the tin.

3. While the pastry is cooking heat the olive oil over a medium heat and fry the onions and bacon, stir occasionally, you will want the onions to be soft and the bacon to be on the light crispy side.

4. Whisk the eggs and milk together with some seasoning.

5. Once the pastry has cooled add the onions and bacon to it, add the cheese on top, then pour over the milk and eggs.

6. Cook in a preheated oven for 20–30 minutes until golden on the top.

TIPS

If you don't have ceramic baking beans, you can use uncooked rice, lentils or dried peas to blind bake the pastry

Use different cheeses with the Cheddar: Emmental, Gruyère or Edam work well. Half and half

Change the bacon for 180g smoked lardons

You can use half full-fat milk and half single cream

Use 1 medium red onion caramelised; slice the onion finely and heat over a medium heat until soft and cooked, add 1 teaspoon sugar and 1 teaspoon balsamic vinegar, and cook for a couple of minutes longer

You can use 180g of ready-made shortcrust pastry instead of making it from scratch if you are short for time

Chicken Fajitas

A great midweek dinner that's simple to make and packed full of flavour. The spice mix in this recipe works well with beef and vegetables – if you can't finish all the fajitas, refrigerate any leftovers and take a wrap for lunch the next day.

Makes 8 fajitas

Ingredients

Fajita spice mix

- 1 tbsp smoked paprika
- 1 tbsp garlic powder
- 1 tbsp oregano
- ½ tbsp cayenne pepper
- 1 tbsp cumin
- 1 tbsp coriander (dried)

Fajitas

- 1–2 tbsp of vegetable oil
- 500g chicken thighs, sliced
- ½ red pepper, sliced
- ½ yellow pepper, sliced
- 1 onion, sliced
- 8 tortillas
- 75g Cheddar cheese, grated
- ½ head of iceberg lettuce, finely sliced
- 150ml soured cream (optional)

Method

1. Add all the spices from the fajita spice mix to a bowl and stir well to combine.

2. Using a frying pan over a medium–hight heat, heat up a tablespoon of the oil until it is just shimmering and add your chicken to the pan. Cook for 6–7 minutes or until the chicken has some good colour to it.

3. Now, add your onion and peppers to the pan along with 1–2 tablespoons of the fajita spice mix and cook for 5–8 minutes or until the vegetables have just softened. (1–2 tablespoons will give you a milder heat but if you want to increase the spice level, just add more of the mix to the pan.)

4. Remove the tortillas from the packaging and add these to a plate covered with cling film and heat in the microwave for 30 seconds.

5. After the tortillas have been warmed through, remove the chicken and vegetables from the heat and transfer to a serving dish and let everyone help themselves at the table.

6. Serve your fajitas alongside the soured cream (if using), Cheddar cheese and lettuce so that everyone can build their own fajitas. You can also serve this alongside a simple salsa and guacamole (see Tips for details).

Make a simple guacamole to serve alongside your fajitas by smashing a large ripe avocado with 1 crushed clove of garlic and the juice of ½ a lime

The spice mix quantities will make more than you need for this recipe and it keeps well in an airtight container for up to 3 months

Make a quick-and-easy salsa by mixing together 3 tomatoes, diced; ½ onion, diced; ½ chill, diced (deseeded if you prefer less heat); 1 garlic clove, finely chopped; and a handful of freshly chopped coriander seasoned with salt just before you serve up the fajitas

You can swap the thighs for chicken breast or thinly cut steak. Alternatively, you can add whole peppers and 350g of mushrooms for a vegetarian-friendly option

Beef Stew
and Dumplings

A rich, hearty stew packed full of melt-in-the-mouth beef and fluffy dumplings.

Serves 6-8

Preheat oven to 150°C/130°C fan/300°F/gas mark 2

Ingredients

- 1 tbsp olive oil
- 700g beef, chuck steak or shin are good cuts to use
- 1 tbsp plain flour
- 1 large onion, chopped
- 2 sticks of celery, sliced
- 3 large carrots, sliced into rounds (approx. 300g)

- 750g potatoes, cut into equal sized pieces (approx. 2 large potatoes)
- 1 garlic clove, crushed
- ½ tsp dried thyme
- ½ tsp dried parsley
- 1 bay leaf
- 2 tbsp tomato purée
- 750ml beef stock

For the dumplings

- 250g self-raising flour
- 125g cold butter

- 4 tbsp of cold water and milk mixed
- salt and pepper, to taste

Method

1. Heat the olive oil in an ovenproof casserole dish. Cut the beef into cubes (5cm) cook the beef until brown on all sides, continue to cook until all the beef is browned. Stir in the flour to cover the beef.

2. Add the rest of the ingredients, stir and bring to the boil. Reduce the heat to a simmer and cook for approx. 1–1½ hours until the beef is tender. If you want a thicker stew you can always add some cornflour, stir and cook until thickened to your liking. Remove the bay leaf.

3. Make the dumplings after the beef has been cooking for about 45–50 minutes.

4. In a mixing bowl add the flour with some salt and pepper. Cut the cold butter into small pieces and rub it into the flour until you have a mixture that looks like breadcrumbs, don't overwork it, keep it light and airy by lifting the flour up while rubbing in the butter, this will create lighter dumplings.

5. Gradually add the cold milk/water to the mixture and with your hands gently bring it to a dough, you may not need to use all the liquid, if you add too much and it is too loose then add some extra flour. Once you have your dough, divide the mixture into approx. 8 portions and create a nice round dumpling by rolling it in your hands gently, makes between 8–10.

6. Remove the beef from the heat and gently drop the dumplings on top, spacing evenly into the stew, cover and continue to cook for another 20–25 minutes until they have increased in size and are cooked. You can test to see if they are cooked by gently inserting a cocktail stick in each one and it comes out clean.

7. Serve with vegetables of your choice.

TIPS

I often prepare all the vegetables and meat the night before and cook it in the slow cooker for about 6–8 hours on low. Add the dumplings for the last hour

You can add some extra flavour to your dumplings by adding herbs (fresh or dried) or some grated cheese to the mixture before adding the liquid

Chilli Con Carne

By no means traditional but oh so tasty – this is great served with rice or used as a filling for the jacket potatoes mentioned earlier.

Serves 4

Ingredients

- 1 tbsp olive oil
- 2 onions, peeled and finely chopped
- 500g beef mince
- 2 garlic cloves, finely chopped
- 1 tsp chilli powder
- 1 tsp ground cumin
- 1 tsp smoked paprika
- 2 tbsp tomato purée
- 1 tbsp brown sugar
- 1 x 400g tin chopped tomatoes
- 300ml beef stock
- 1 x 400g tin kidney beans
- 1 x 200g tin baked beans
- 4 squares of good-quality (75% cocoa) dark chocolate

Method

1. Heat a tablespoon of olive oil in a large non-stick frying pan and gently cook the onions for 10 minutes or until softened. Once cooked, remove from the pan and set to one side.

2. In the same pan, cook the mince over a medium–high heat to brown for 8–10 minutes, stirring occasionally so that it doesn't burn.

3. After the meat has some good colour to it, add the onions back to the pan, along with the chilli powder, ground cumin and smoked paprika. Cook until fragrant.

4. Add the tomato purée and sugar to the pan, cook for 1–2 minutes before reducing the temperature to a medium heat and adding the garlic to the pan and cooking for another minute.

5. Throw in the tin of chopped tomatoes along with the beef stock, stirring to combine everything, before bringing to the boil. Reduce the heat and simmer for 30 minutes. Add both tins of beans to the pan after 20 minutes. Once the cooking has finished, turn off the heat and stir through the chocolate for a lovely, velvety rich flavour.

6. Serve with rice or jacket potatoes (see page 27) before grating on a load of Cheddar cheese for that classic canteen taste. Yum!

(V) For a vegan-friendly option, either substitute the beef mince for 500g of a meat alternative or add an additional 3 x 200g tins of pulses (butter beans, chickpeas, mixed beans), plus 1 large carrot and 1 small red pepper, chopped.

TIPS

You could also try serving this with freshly chopped coriander and chilli, a dollop of soured cream and a squeeze of lime

Chilli always tastes better the next day after the flavours have had the chance to become friends

Cheese and Onion Pie

Savoury and satisfying, cheese and onion pie was one of the few vegetarian options at school that everyone loved.

Serves 6-8

Preheat oven to 200°C/180°C fan/400°F/gas mark 6

Ingredients

- 1 x 320g pack of ready-made shortcrust pastry
- 40g butter
- 4–5 large onions, finely sliced
- 1 tsp sugar
- 1 tsp thyme
- 150ml cold water
- 200g Lancashire cheese, grated
- 100g mature Cheddar cheese, grated
- 1 egg yolk
- salt and pepper, to taste

Method

1. Roll out the pastry and line a 20 x 20xcm pie dish with it. Prick the bottom of the pastry and leave it to one side, ensuring that there is enough leftover to make the top for your pie.

2. In a large pan melt the butter and add the onions, sprinkle the sugar, thyme and salt and pepper onto the onions and cook over a low–medium heat until they are softened and translucent. Add the water and continue to cook until all the water has evaporated, approx. 15 mins. Remove from the pan and leave to cool for about 10–15 minutes.

3. Grate the cheeses and mix together. Once the onions have cooled put half onto the base of the pastry and then cover with half the cheeses, then repeat.

4. Roll out the rest of your pastry for the top, slightly dampen the edges of the pastry around the rim of the dish and then place your pastry top on, with your finger and thumb press together the edges, make a couple of small slits (about 2cm) in the top to allow the steam to escape to give you a flat top when baked. Brush with some of the egg yolk.

5. Cook in the preheated oven for 15 minutes, then reduce the temperature to 180°C/160°C fan/350°F/gas mark 4 for another 25 minutes until light golden brown.

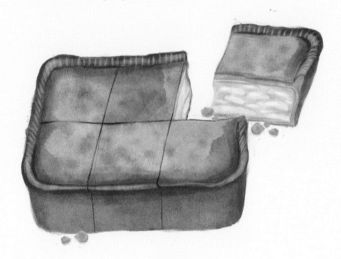

Serve with mashed potatoes/chips and baked beans

It can be served hot or cold

For a vegan alternative, use dairy alternatives for the butter, milk and cheeses

Beef and Potato Pie

*Hearty and filling – perfect with a healthy helping
of gravy and another form of potato, of course.*

Serves 4-6

Preheat oven to 160°C/140°C fan/325°F/gas mark 3

Ingredients

- 500g beef stewing or braising steak, cut into 1-inch cubes
- 2 tbsp plain flour
- salt and pepper, to season
- 2 ½ tbsp vegetable oil
- 1 large onion, diced
- 2 carrots, peeled and sliced
- 2 garlic cloves, crushed
- 2 tsp fresh thyme leaves (or 1 tsp dried thyme)

- 1 bay leaf
- 230ml beef stock
- 230ml red wine (or additional beef stock)
- 4 medium potatoes, peeled and cut into 1-inch cubes
- 1 x 500g block of ready-made puff pastry
- 1 egg, beaten with 1 tbsp water

Method

1. Pop the flour and a little salt and pepper into a plastic bag (resealable to avoid any escaping flour) and shake to mix, then add the beef and coat it with the flour.

2. Heat 2 tbsp of the vegetable oil in a large frying pan over medium–high heat and brown the beef cubes in batches. Transfer the browned beef to a plate and set aside.

3. Using the same frying pan sauté the onion and carrots until softened, add the remaining ½ tbsp of vegetable oil if needed, cook for about 5 minutes. Add the garlic and thyme, and cook

for 1 more minute.

4. Return the beef to the pan and add the bay leaf, beef stock and red wine (or additional stock). Taste and add more salt and black pepper if needed.

5. Bring the mixture to a simmer, then transfer to an ovenproof dish, cover and bake in the preheated oven for approx. 1–1½ hours.

6. While the beef is cooking prepare the potatoes, parboil in hot water for no longer than 3–5 minutes on a medium heat, remove and drain, leave in the pan until ready to add to the beef.

7. Remove the beef from the oven and discard the bay leaf then stir in the parboiled cubed potatoes.

8. On a lightly floured surface, roll out the puff pastry to the depth of a £1 coin and so that it fits on top of the pot with a slight overhang (you might not need all the pastry). Brush the edges of the pot with some of the egg and water mixture and place the puff pastry over the top, pressing the edges to seal. Make a couple of slits in the top of the pastry to allow the steam to escape while cooking.

9. Brush the top of the pastry with the remaining egg wash. Increase the oven to 200°C/180°C fan/400°F/gas mark 6, return the pie to the oven and bake for another 30–40 minutes until the pastry is golden brown and risen.

10. Allow the pie to rest for approx. 10 minutes before serving.

TIPS

Get ahead by using a slow cooker to cook the beef filling the day before. After searing the beef, simply add all the ingredients to the pot and cook on low for 6–6½ hours

Add frozen peas or other vegetables to the filling for extra nutrition

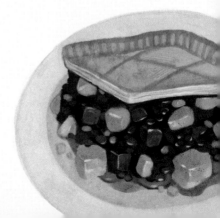

Chicken, Leek and Mushroom Pie

A classic, puff pastry-topped pie packed with juicy bits of chicken, sweet leek and onion that is perfect as a midweek dinner. (No mystery meat here!)

Serves 4-6

Preheat the oven to 180°C/160°C fan/350°F/gas mark 4

Ingredients

- 2–3 rashers of bacon (smoked lardons add more flavour)
- 1 tbsp olive oil, for frying
- 500g chicken thighs, diced into 1-inch chunks
- 1 leek, halved and sliced
- 1 onion, sliced
- 150g mushrooms, sliced
- 2–3 garlic cloves, chopped
- 1 tsp thyme
- 5 tbsp butter

- 4 tbsp plain flour
- 500ml chicken stock
- 1 tsp Dijon mustard
- handful of fresh parsley, chopped
- squeeze of lemon
- 1 x 320g packet of ready-made puff pastry
- 1 egg, beaten with a little water to loosen it
- salt and pepper, to taste

Method

1. Add the bacon to a cold frying pan and turn the pan onto a medium heat to slowly render out the fat. After 8–10 minutes, the bacon will be nice and crispy. Using a slotted spoon, so that the bacon fat remains in the pan, transfer the crispy bacon to a paper towel-lined plate to soak up any excess fat.

2. In the same pan, add a little oil and increase the heat to medium–high

before adding the chicken thighs and cooking for around 10 minutes. Once cooked and well browned, remove the chicken from the pan with a slotted spoon and reserve any meat juices in a separate bowl.

3. Reduce the heat to medium and add the leek and onion. After 5 minutes, when the leek and onion has started to soften, add the sliced mushroom and cook for another 5 minutes.

4. Move the vegetables to one side of the pan and add your garlic to the centre of the pan. Cook the garlic for around a minute, or until fragrant, before bringing the vegetables back into the mix and allowing the flavour to get to know one another. Add the thyme, cooking for another minute before removing from the heat.

5. As your filling sits to the side, melt the butter in a pan over a medium heat and cook until melted and just bubbling. Add the flour and cook this out for a couple of minutes until you are left with a loose paste.

6. Once all the flour is incorporated and you've cooked it off for a couple of minutes, add around a third of the chicken stock and whisk continuously until combined, much like you would with a roux (page 49). Continue adding the remaining stock a third at a time until you are left with a thick, chicken stock-based sauce.

7. Turn off the heat, add the reserved meat juices and Dijon mustard to the sauce, season well and stir to combine.

8. Return the chicken and bacon to the vegetables, add the parsley and a squeeze of lemon before pouring over the sauce. Stir together and place the filling into a pie dish.

9. Remove the pastry from the fridge. You can use a rolling pin to make the pastry thinner but check the unrolled piece against your pie dish before you roll it out. You are looking for around the thickness of a £1 coin. Place the pastry lid on top of the filling, brush with the egg and season with salt.

10. Put your pie in the oven to bake for 30–35 minutes, turning halfway through, until you have a crispy, golden-brown topping.

Shepherd's Pie

A comforting classic, shepherd's pie is a go-to staple in many homes and schools across the country – simple and satisfying.

Serves 4-6

Preheat oven to 200°C/180°C fan/400°F/gas mark 6

Ingredients

- 800g potatoes
- 1 tbsp olive oil
- 1 large onion, finely chopped
- 2 sticks of celery, finely chopped
- 2 carrots, peeled and finely chopped
- 500g lamb mince
- 2 tbsp plain flour

- 1 tsp dried rosemary
- 1 tsp dried thyme
- 450ml lamb stock
- 2 tbsp Worcestershire sauce (optional)
- 50–100ml milk
- 1–2 tbsp butter
- salt and pepper, to taste

Method

1. Peel the potatoes and cut into quarters, add to a pan of cold water, just enough to cover, and gently bring to the boil, simmer until the potatoes are just soft on the inside. Remove from the heat and drain, leave in the pan with lid slightly covering the pan, allows the potatoes to steam a little which will help when mashing to make the topping.

2. Heat the olive oil in a large non-stick frying pan and gently cook the vegetables for approx. 10 minutes on a medium heat until the onion is softened. Remove and set aside until later.

3. In the same frying pan add the lamb mince, rosemary and thyme over a medium heat to brown, stirring occasionally so that it does

not burn. Once the lamb has some good colour, stir in the flour and add the vegetables back to the pan. Crumble the stock cube over the mince, add 450ml of boiling water and the Worcestershire sauce. Give it all a jolly good stir! Bring to the boil and simmer for 15–20 minutes, stirring occasionally, until the liquid has reduced.

4. Remove from the heat and allow to cool while making the topping.

5. Mash the potatoes, adding the milk and butter slowly until you have the right consistency, they should not be too smooth and should be able to hold their own. However, if you wish to pipe the potato on the top then they will need to be a little smoother.

6. I often use the same dish that I do for the lasagne recipe, which I find is a perfect size! Add the lamb to the dish, cover with the mashed potato, smoothing it over to cover the lamb. Use a fork to fluff up the potato topping so that you get a lovely crispy edge once it is cooked.

7. Pop it into the oven for 25–35 minutes until lovely and golden brown on the top.

8. Serve with vegetables, such as peas, broccoli and carrots.

TIPS

Add some grated Cheddar cheese to the potato

Add mustard instead of the Worcestershire sauce

Once cooled, cut into portions, and freeze for those days when you feel like a warming Shepherd's Pie

Sweet Treats

Recipes

Stick-To-Your-Teeth Chocolate Brownies

Fudgy, oozy goodness that's worth the extra flossing.

Makes 10–12

Preheat oven to 180°C/160°C fan/350°F/gas mark 4

Ingredients

- 200g dark chocolate, roughly chopped
- 200g butter
- 4 large eggs
- 300g granulated sugar
- 1 tsp vanilla extract

- 1 egg white
- ¼ tsp salt
- 150g plain flour
- 100g chopped walnuts or pecans (optional)

Method

1. Grease and line a 20cm square tin with baking parchment, leaving an overhang on two sides for easy removal.

2. Melt the chocolate and butter in a heatproof bowl over a saucepan of simmering water. Stir occasionally until smooth and well combined. Remove from the heat and set aside to cool slightly.

3. Whisk the eggs, sugar, vanilla extract and salt in a separate bowl or electric mixer until it is well combined, light and slightly thickened.

4. Use a separate bowl to whisk the egg white until peaks form.

5. Gently fold the cooled melted chocolate mixture into the egg mixture along with the egg white until combined.

6. Sift the flour and fold gently until just combined, do not over-mix. Gently fold in the chopped nuts, if using.

7. Pour the brownie batter into the prepared tin and spread evenly.

8. Bake for 20–25 minutes, until the top is set and a toothpick inserted in the centre comes out with a few moist crumbs attached.

9. Remove from the oven and let cool completely in the tin before cutting into squares.

TIPS

For an extra fudgy texture, underbake the brownies slightly

Once removed from the oven the brownies will continue to cook slightly so if you want a more moist brownie then remove from the oven (depending on your oven temperature) about 2 minutes before the end of the cooking time

For a different flavour use milk or white chocolate

Add a teaspoon of instant coffee powder or espresso to enhance the chocolate flavour

Serve warm with a scoop of vanilla ice cream or a drizzle of caramel sauce

Can be made ahead and stored in an airtight container for up to 5 days

When lining the tin with the baking parchment, hold along the edges to keep it secure with plastic pegs, remove before filling and baking

While the chocolate is melting, save time by whisking the eggs, sugar etc., and the egg white

Butterscotch Tart

*Sweet and nostalgic – one of the
very best, classic canteen desserts!*

Serves 8

Preheat oven to 180°C/160°C fan/350°F/gas mark 4

Ingredients

For the pastry

- 225g plain flour
- 110g butter,
  chilled and cubed
- 1 egg yolk
- 2–3 tbsp cold water

For the butterscotch filling

- 100g butter
- 100g light brown sugar
- 2 tbsp golden syrup
- 300ml double cream
- 1 tsp vanilla extract

Method

Pastry

1. Grease a 23cm tart tin.

2. Rub the butter into the flour until it resembles breadcrumbs (this
   can be done either by hand or with an electric mixer).

3. Add the egg yolk and cold water, pulsing until the dough comes
   together. Shape the pastry into a flat circle and wrap in cling film,
   chill in the fridge for 30 minutes.

4. Roll out the pastry on a floured surface and line the tart tin. Prick

the base with a fork and chill for 15 minutes.

5. Line the pastry with baking parchment and fill with baking beans. Bake blind for 15 minutes, then remove the beans and parchment and bake for a further 5 minutes until golden. Allow to cool.

Butterscotch filling

6. In a saucepan, melt the butter, light brown sugar, and golden syrup over low heat, stirring until smooth.

7. Slowly pour in the double cream while stirring continuously.

8. Bring the mixture to a gentle simmer on a low heat and cook for 5–7 minutes, stirring constantly, until thickened.

9. Remove from heat, stir in the vanilla extract, and allow to cool slightly.

10. Pour the warm butterscotch filling into the cooled pastry case.

11. Smooth the top with a spatula and refrigerate for at least 2 hours to set.

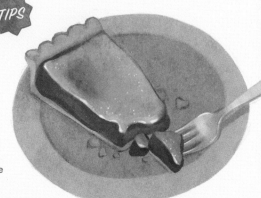

TIPS

Sprinkle a pinch of sea salt over the butterscotch filling for a different flavour

Serve the butterscotch tart chilled, with cream or ice cream

Dust with a little icing sugar before serving for a decorative touch

Can be made ahead of time and stored in the fridge until ready to serve

If short on time use a ready-made sweet pastry case

Chocolate Pudding and Pink Custard

A retro classic that's as fun as it is delicious, bringing back those school dessert memories.

Makes 8-10 portions

Preheat oven to 180°C/160°C fan/350°F/gas mark 4

Ingredients

- 200g self-raising flour
- 50g cocoa powder
- 150g caster sugar
- 100g butter, softened

- 2 large eggs
- 150ml milk
- 1 tsp vanilla extract

For the custard

- 500ml whole milk
- 50g caster sugar
- 3 large egg yolks

- 1 tsp vanilla extract
- 2–3 drops of red food colouring

Method

1. Grease a 20cm square baking tin.

2. For the pudding, sift the flour and cocoa powder in a large bowl, then stir in the sugar, mix it to combine together.

3. Add the rest of the pudding ingredients and mix well until it is smooth using an electric mixer.

4. Pour the mixture into the greased baking tin and bake for

approximately 30–35 minutes, test to make sure the pudding is cooked.

5. Let the pudding cool slightly while you make the pink custard.

Pink custard

6. In a saucepan heat the milk and sugar over a medium heat, stirring occasionally until the sugar has dissolved.

7. Use a separate bowl to whisk the egg yolks until they are light and creamy, then take your hot milk and slowly pour onto the egg yolks whisking all the time, continuing doing this until all the milk has been used and the custard is smooth.

8. Now pour the mixture back into the saucepan and cook the mixture over a low-medium heat stirring constantly until it thickens, be patient! It will happen, you are looking for the mixture to coat the back of the spoon.

9. Take the pan off the heat and stir in the vanilla extract and food colouring (add the food colouring a little at a time until you get the colour you desire).

10. Pour the warm pink custard over the chocolate pudding.

TIPS

You can use the above custard method to make a plain vanilla custard, just leave out the food colouring

The custard can be made before the pudding and then you can reheat it, personally I prefer it just made

The chocolate sponge can be frozen and defrosted when needed and re-heated

94

Chocolate Concrete Crunch

Chocolatey, crunchy goodness that is great as a little pick-me-up treat in the week!

Makes 8 portions

Ingredients

- 200g digestive biscuits
- 100g butter
- 3 tbsp golden syrup
- 200g milk chocolate, broken into pieces
- 100g plain chocolate, broken into pieces
- 2 tbsp vegetable oil
- 100g puffed rice

Method

1. Line a 20cm square baking tin with baking parchment or grease it lightly with butter.

2. Crush the digestive biscuits until they form fine crumbs. You can do this in a food processor or you can put the biscuits in a resealable bag and crush them with a rolling pin.

3. In a saucepan over a low heat melt the butter and golden syrup, stirring occasionally, until combined. Once combined, remove the mixture from the heat and stir in the crushed digestive biscuits until well combined.

4. Press the biscuit mixture firmly and evenly into the prepared baking tin before refrigerating for 30 minutes.

5. In a heatproof bowl set over a saucepan of simmering water, melt

the milk chocolate and plain chocolate together, stirring occasionally, until smooth and well combined.

6. Remove the chocolate from the heat and stir in the vegetable oil until fully incorporated.

7. Add the puffed rice until well coated and evenly distributed in the chocolate mixture.

8. Evenly spread the chocolate-cereal mixture over the chilled biscuit base and then refrigerate the chocolate concrete crunch for at least 2 hours. (If you can wait, it's even better left overnight!)

9. Once set, remove the chocolate crunch from the tin and cut into squares.

Add some chopped nuts or crushed honeycomb to the chocolate-cereal mixture

Drizzle with melted white chocolate or dust with icing sugar for a decorative touch

Use dark or white chocolate for a different flavour variation

Can be made in advance and stored in an airtight container for up to 5 days

Manchester Tart

Coconut and jam goodness that's as northern and comforting as tea round your nan's house.

Makes 8 portions

Preheat oven to 180°C/160°C fan/350°F/gas mark 4

Ingredients

For the pastry

- 225g plain flour
- 110g butter, chilled and cubed
- 2–3 tbsp cold water

For the filling

- 500ml whole milk
- 2 eggs
- 100g caster sugar
- 2 tbsp cornflour
- 1 tsp vanilla extract
- 4–5 tbsp raspberry jam
- 50g desiccated coconut

Method

Pastry

1. Grease a 23cm pie dish and set aside.

2. Rub the flour and butter together to resemble breadcrumbs (you can use an electric mixer to do this), add the cold water a tablespoon at a time until the dough just comes together.

3. Shape the pastry into a flat circle and wrap in cling film, chill in the fridge for 30 minutes.

4. Roll out the chilled pastry to fit the pie dish and line it with the pastry

and trim the edges. Set to one side until you make the filling.

Filling

5. In a saucepan, heat the milk over medium heat until just simmering.

6. In a separate bowl, whisk together the eggs, sugar and cornflour until pale in colour.

7. Slowly pour the hot milk into the egg mixture, whisking constantly.

8. Return the mixture to the saucepan and cook, stirring continuously over a medium-low heat, until thickened to a custard-like consistency, this can take about 5 minutes.

9. Remove from the heat and stir in the vanilla extract. Allow to cool slightly.

10. While the filling is cooling spread the raspberry jam evenly over the pastry base.

11. Pour the slightly cooled custard filling over the jam, sprinkle the desiccated coconut evenly over the top.

12. Bake in the preheated oven for 30–35 minutes, until the pastry is golden brown.

13. Allow to cool slightly before serving.

TIPS

Use a combination of butter and lard for a richer pastry

Use different jam flavours, such as strawberry, blackberry or cherry

Serve warm or chilled, with cream, custard or ice cream

This dish can be made in advance and reheated before serving

Sticky Toffee Pudding

*Warm, gooey delight that's like a
comforting hug in dessert form.*

Makes 8 portions

Preheat the oven to 200°C/180°C fan/400°F/gas mark 6

Ingredients

- 55g butter, softened
- 170g demerara sugar
- 290ml boiling water
- 200g pitted dates, chopped
- 2 eggs

- 200g self-raising flour
- 1 tbsp golden syrup
- 2 tbsp black treacle
- 1 tsp bicarbonate of soda
- 1/2 tsp vanilla extract

For the toffee sauce

- 110g butter
- 110g muscovado sugar

- 210ml double cream
- 1 tsp vanilla extract

Method

1. Line a 20 cm square baking tin with baking parchment.

2. Cream the butter and sugar together until it is mixed, approximately 5 minutes.

3. Pour the boiling water over the dates and set aside for a few minutes.

4. Add the eggs, syrup and black treacle to the butter and sugar and continue mixing until all the ingredients have come together and it's a lovely caramel colour.

5. Add the flour to the mixture until all blended.

6. Using either a liquidiser or stick blender, blend the dates and water together for a few minutes to make a purée. Add the bicarbonate of soda and vanilla extract and stir, then add this to the rest of the ingredients and mix well until everything is blended.

7. Pour the mixture into the prepared tin and cook in the oven for approximately 20-25 minutes until golden brown.

8. To make the toffee sauce, melt all the ingredients, except the vanilla extract, in a saucepan over a medium heat stirring constantly until the sugar has dissolved and then add the vanilla extract continue stirring until the sauce thickens slightly.

9. Serve warm with a drizzle of the toffee sauce.

TIPS

You could always serve this pudding without the
toffee sauce and substitute it with a custard (Why not both?)

Both the pudding and sauce can be frozen.
However, it is easier to freeze them separately

Apple Crumble

Sweet, crumbly and warming – it's a classic!

Makes 4-6 portions

Preheat oven to 190°C/170°C fan/375°F/gas mark 5

Ingredients

- 3 large baking apples
- (about 850g–900g in total)
- grated rind and juice of 1 lemon
- 3 tbsp water

- 50g caster sugar
- 80g cold butter
- 180g plain flour
- 80g golden caster sugar

Method

1. Peel, core and chop the apples into chunks. Put them in a saucepan and pour over the lemon juice, add the water and the 50g of sugar, gently stir to mix. Simmer gently on low heat for approximately 5 minutes remove from the heat and leave in the pan to cool.

2. Rub the butter into the flour until the mixture resembles breadcrumbs, stir in the golden caster sugar.

3. Your apple should now be cool and should have a lovely syrup coating. Gently put the apples in the bottom of an ovenproof dish and then the crumble on the top.

4. Bake in the preheated oven for approximately 20–25 minutes until the crumble is a light golden colour.

TIPS

Can be served with custard,
ice cream or cream

If you have an eating apple,
which is just not getting eaten,
then use this in your apple filling

Suitable for freezing

Rice Pudding

Creamy and comforting, like a warm
blanket and a good book on a rainy day.

Serves 4-6

Preheat oven to 150°C/130°C fan/300°F/gas mark 2

Ingredients

- 100g short grain pudding rice
- 1l whole milk
- 50g caster sugar
- 1 tsp vanilla extract
- 1 tsp cinnamon
- 1 tsp dried nutmeg (or ½ tsp of freshly grated nutmeg)
- pinch of salt

Method

1. Use a large ovenproof dish and combine all the ingredients together, except the nutmeg.

2. Stir the mixture well to ensure the sugar has dissolved.

3. Sprinkle the nutmeg over the top and cover the dish with a lid or foil and bake in the preheated oven for 2–2½ hours, stirring occasionally, remove the lid/foil and cook uncovered for the last 30 minutes until the rice is tender and the pudding has thickened and has a lovely skin on the top.

4. Serve the rice pudding warm, with a sprinkle of extra nutmeg or cinnamon on top, if desired.

Dollop a tablespoon of jam on top for that classic school taste

Drizzle some golden syrup over the top or add a sprinkle of desiccated coconut

This dish can be made in advance and reheated before serving

You can freeze this by placing single portions into bags and lying them flat in the freezer, use within 3 months, defrost thoroughly before use

To make this vegan, use a plant- or nut-based milk

Jam Roly-Poly

*Rolled up with love, this pudding
is a sweet trip down memory lane.*

Serves 8-10

Preheat oven to 180°C/160°C fan/350°F/gas mark 4

Ingredients

- 225g self-raising flour
- 70g vegetable suet
- 40g butter
- pinch of salt
- 150ml cold water
- 4–5 tbsp jam of your choice

Method

1. Grease a large baking sheet or line it with baking parchment.

2. In a large bowl, mix together the flour, suet, butter and a pinch of salt. Gradually add the cold water, mixing until a soft dough forms.

3. On a lightly floured surface, roll the dough out into a large rectangle approximately 30cm x 20cm.

4. Spread the jam evenly over the dough, leaving a 2–3cm border around the edges.

5. Carefully roll up the dough from the long side to enclose the jam.

6. Put the rolled-up jam roly-poly onto the prepared baking sheet, the join should be underneath.

7. Bake in the preheated oven for 25–30 minutes, until the pastry is golden brown.

8. Let it cool slightly and dust the top with a little icing sugar before serving.

TIPS

You can use all suet
instead of the butter

Serve warm with
custard or ice cream

Can be made in advance and
warmed in the oven when ready

Bread and Butter Pudding

Simple, sweet, and oh-so-comforting,
like the best of childhood desserts.

Serves 4

Preheat oven to 180°C/160°C fan/350°F/gas mark 4

Ingredients

- 3 eggs
- 400ml milk
- 200ml double cream
- 1 tsp vanilla extract
- nutmeg, grated
- 8–10 slices bread

- 40g butter, softened
- 3 tbsp golden caster sugar
- 70g raisins
- grated zest of 1 lemon
- 20g demerara sugar

Method

1. Whisk the eggs, milk and cream together, stir in the vanilla extract and a little grating of nutmeg.

2. Cut the crusts off the bread and feed the birds with them or blitz them to make breadcrumbs. Butter both sides of the bread with the butter and cut into triangles.

3. Mix the raisins with the golden caster sugar and zest of lemon.

4. In a 20cm square ovenproof dish put one layer of buttered triangles in, then half the raisins over, and then repeat.

5. Pour over the whisked egg mixture to cover the bread and leave for about 30 minutes to allow the bread to soak up the mixture.

6. Sprinkle the demerara sugar over the top and cook in the preheated oven for 30–35 minutes until light golden brown in colour.

TIPS

If you prefer use orange instead of the lemon

Serve warm with ice cream, custard or cream

Easy to freeze in portions, defrost before reheating

Stale bread is fine to use, but you could use brioche, brown or white bread

Lemon Drizzle Cake

*Zesty and sweet, a cake that's as bright
and cheerful as a summer's day.*

Makes 8-10 portions

Preheat oven to 180°C/160°C fan/350°F/gas mark 4

Ingredients

- 180g butter, softened
- 180g caster sugar
- 2 eggs
- 180g self-raising flour, sifted
- 4 tbsp milk
- grated rind and juice
  of 1 large unwaxed lemon
- 100g caster sugar

Method

1. Line a 20cm square cake tin with baking parchment.

2. Cream the butter, 180g caster sugar and lemon rind together until light and fluffy.

3. Whisk the eggs together and then slowly add to the mixture, add a tablespoon of flour if the mixture starts to curdle.

4. Fold in the flour gently, add in the milk and mix together.

5. Put the mixture into the prepared tin and bake in the preheated oven for approximately 30–35 minutes until the cake springs back when lightly pressed.

6. While the cake is cooking put the lemon juice and 100g caster sugar into a pan on a low heat stirring until the sugar has dissolved, the mixture should have a syrupy consistency, keep your eye on it!

7. Once out of the oven, make random holes using a toothpick or

skewer over the top and then pour the lovely lemon syrup over letting it sink into the holes you've made. Sprinkle some sugar over the top for an extra crunch. Let the cake cool completely and then cut into equal squares.

The cake can be wrapped and frozen as it freezes well, I do this in portions and grab one for a treat with a lovely cup of coffee or tea!

You can also add a lovely lemon icing by using 50g icing sugar and approx. juice ½ a lemon, mix together and drizzle over the cake. Add some lemon rind for decoration

Chocolate Crispy Cakes

*Gooey, crunchy bites that take
you right back to school.*

Makes 12

Ingredients

- 50g butter
- 50g milk chocolate,
  broken into pieces
- 50g dark chocolate,
  broken into pieces

- 5 tbsp golden syrup
- ½ tsp vanilla extract
- 100g corn flakes

You will need 12 standard paper cases

Method

1. In a large saucepan melt the butter over a low heat. Once melted remove from the heat and stir in the milk and dark chocolate pieces until it is completely melted and smooth.

2. Add the golden syrup and vanilla extract to the chocolate mixture and stir until well combined.

3. Fold in the corn flakes, gently mixing until all the cereal is evenly coated with the chocolate mixture.

4. Transfer the mixture into the paper cases evenly.

5. Refrigerate for at least an hour before serving to set.

TIPS

Use a microwave to melt the
butter and chocolate separately,
continue as above

Keep in an airtight container
in the fridge for up to 5 days

Before putting in the fridge to set,
decorate with a chocolate mini egg
(or three) on each crispy cake

Toffee and Marshmallow Squares

*Sticky, sweet, and fun –
don't eat them all at once.*

Makes 12-16 portions

Ingredients

- 110g toffees
- 110g butter

- 110g marshmallows
- 110g puffed rice

Method

1. Melt the toffees, butter and marshmallows in a non-stick pan over a low heat, ensuring that you stir the mixture constantly until it's a light caramel colour. This should take 4–5 minutes.

2. Once melted, remove the pan from the heat and mix in the puffed rice so that each crispy morsel is covered in the sticky, tasty mixture.

3. Refrigerate the mixture in a lined 25cm x 8cm baking tray for a minimum of 2 hours before removing and cutting into equal-sized pieces (as big or as small as you'd like!)

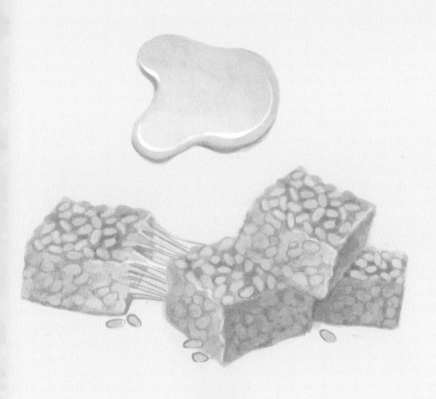

You can use different quantities, smaller
or larger, but just adjust the size of
your tin to accommodate

Millionaire's Shortbread

Rich layers of indulgence that taste
like a fortune of sweet memories.

Makes 8-10 portions

Preheat oven to 180°C/160°C fan/350°F/gas mark 4

Ingredients

For the shortbread

- 100g caster sugar
- 200g butter
  at room temperature
- 275g plain flour

For the caramel filling

- 1 x 397g tin sweetened
  condensed milk
- 200g butter
- 40g caster sugar
- 100g golden syrup

For the chocolate topping

- 250g dark chocolate
- 100g white chocolate

Method

Shortbread

1. Grease or line the bottom of a 20cm square baking tin.

2. Cream together the caster sugar and butter until light and smooth, add the flour until it forms a soft dough.

3. Press the shortbread mixture evenly into the prepared tin and bake in the pre-heated oven for 20–25 minutes until pale golden in colour, remove from the oven and leave to go cold.

Caramel

4. In a non-stick saucepan add the condensed milk, butter, sugar and golden syrup, and stir constantly over a low heat to combine the ingredients for the filling.

5. Turn the heat up to high and bring to the boil, stirring constantly for about 6–8 minutes until the mixture has thickened and turned a deep caramel colour. (The mixture will be very hot so be careful while stirring.)

6. Once the mixture is ready, pour evenly onto the cold shortbread base put it into the fridge to set. It can be left in the fridge overnight and the topping done the following day.

7. Once set, remove the caramel-topped shortbread base from the fridge and make your chocolate topping.

Chocolate topping

8. In two separate heatproof bowls over a pan of simmering water, add the white and dark chocolate, stirring occasionally until smooth. (Alternatively, use a microwave to melt the chocolate.)

9. Once melted, pour the dark chocolate over the set caramel base for an even coating.

10. While the dark chocolate is unset, randomly dollop pools of the melted white chocolate across the top before swirling this into the dark to create a marble effect.

11. Put it into the fridge for at least 2 hours, or until the chocolate has set.

Can be made in advance and stored in the fridge until ready to serve, remove from the fridge about 30 minutes before serving

Victoria Sponge Cake

*Classic, elegant and the perfect
partner to a cup of tea.*

Makes 8 portions

Preheat oven to 190°C/170°C fan/375°F/gas mark 5

Ingredients

- 175g butter
- 175g caster sugar
- 1 tsp vanilla essence

- 175g self-raising flour
- 1 tsp baking powder
- 3 eggs

For the filling

- 250g icing sugar, sieved
- 90g butter
- ½ tsp vanilla essence

- 30ml milk
- approx. 1 tbsp jam
  (strawberry or raspberry)

Method

1. Grease and line 2 x 20cm cake tins.

2. Cream the butter, sugar and vanilla essence together until pale in colour.

3. Sieve the flour and baking powder together.

4. In a separate bowl whisk the eggs together.

5. Add approximately ⅓ of the egg to the creamed butter and one tablespoon of flour, continue mixing, continue adding the egg and flour until it is all combined, do not over-mix.

6. Transfer the mixture and divide between the cake tins, then smooth

down with a flat-sided knife.

7. Bake for 20 minutes in the preheated oven until the top springs back when gently pressed and they are golden brown in colour.

8. Allow to cool in the tins and then turn them out onto a wire rack to go cold.

9. Once the cakes are cold spread the jam over one of the cakes and buttercream (refer to the instructions on page 121) on the other, sandwich together, then sieve some icing sugar over the top.

You can use lemon curd instead of jam and replace the vanilla essence with a few drops of lemon essence into the buttercream

Any leftover buttercream can be frozen for up to 3 months in the freezer, defrost overnight in the fridge before use

Corn Flake Tart

*Crunchy and sweet, this tart is the
perfect reminder of your school days.*

Makes 8 portions

Preheat oven to 190°C/170°C fan/375°F/gas mark 5

Ingredients

For the pastry

- 200g plain flour
- 100g cold butter, cubed
- 2–3 tbsp cold water

For the filling

- 100g butter
- 100g golden syrup
- 100g light brown sugar
- 120g corn flakes
- 1 tsp vanilla extract
- ¼ tsp ground cinnamon (optional)
- 2–2½ tbsp jam (strawberry or raspberry)

Method

1. To make the pastry, rub the cold butter into the flour until it resembles breadcrumbs. Add the cold water a little at a time and knead into a dough. Wrap the dough in cling film and chill in the fridge for about 30 minutes.

2. Roll out the pastry and line a 20cm loose-bottomed tart tin or pie dish (lightly greased). Prick the base with a fork and put some crunched up tin foil over the bottom of the pastry and top with baking beans, bake blind for 10 minutes. Remove the baking beans and bake for 5 more minutes until lightly golden. Leave to cool in the tin.

3. Once cooled, spread the jam over the bottom of the pastry.

4. In a non-stick saucepan, melt the butter, golden syrup, and brown sugar over medium heat, stirring frequently until the sugar has dissolved and the mixture is smooth.

5. Remove from heat and stir in the corn flakes, vanilla extract, and cinnamon (if using) until well coated.

6. Spoon the corn flake mixture onto the pre-baked pastry case and spread evenly, then sprinkle a handful of corn flakes over the top for an extra crunch.

7. Bake for 10–15 minutes until the filling is bubbling and lightly browned on top.

8. Allow the tart to cool completely before slicing and serving.

Drizzle with melted chocolate or dust with icing sugar for an added touch

Serve warm or at room temperature with a dollop of whipped cream or custard

Can be made in advance and keeps well for several days

Adjust the amount of golden syrup to your desired level of sweetness

If you don't have baking beans use dried rice or dried lentils

Chocolate Cake

Rich, indulgent, creamy and oh so chocolatey.

Makes 8 portions

Preheat oven to 180°C/160°C fan/350°F/gas mark 4

Ingredients

- 200g self-raising flour
- 225g caster sugar
- 1/2 tsp salt
- 25g cocoa powder
- 115g butter

- 2 eggs
- 75ml evaporated milk
- 5 tbsp water
- ½ tsp vanilla essence

For the filling

- 250g icing sugar, sieved
- 90g butter

- 30g cocoa powder
- 30ml milk

Method

1. Sieve the flour, sugar, salt and cocoa powder together.

2. Rub in the butter until you have a breadcrumb-like consistency.

3. Whisk the eggs and evaporated milk together, stir this into the mixture with the water and vanilla essence, beat well to incorporate.

4. Divide the mixture between 2 x 20cm lined tins and bake in a preheated oven for approximately 25–30 minutes, test with a skewer or fork until it comes out clean, the cake should spring back when pressed gently on the top.

5. Allow the cake to go cold before adding the filling.

6. Mix together the sieved icing sugar, butter and cocoa powder until it is well mixed. Add the milk to the mixture slowly and then continue mixing until you have a light fluffy buttercream.

7. Dust the top of the cake with some icing sugar with a sieve.

TIPS

Melt some milk chocolate and pour over the top of the cake, while still hot make some marks with a fork, or crumble over some chocolate flakes

If you have any buttercream left over this can be frozen until you need it, pop it into a container or freezer bag and defrost for 24 hours in the fridge before needed

Sprinkle Cake

Everyone's favourite!

Makes 8-10 portions

Preheat oven to 180°C/160°C fan/350°F/gas mark 4

Ingredients

- 180g butter, softened
- 180g caster sugar
- 2 eggs
- ¼ tsp vanilla essence
- 4 tbsp milk
- 180g self-raising flour, sifted

For the topping

- 180g–200g icing sugar
- sprinkles

Method

1. Line a 20cm square cake tin with baking parchment.

2. Cream the butter and sugar together until it is light and pale (an electric whisk will make light work of this).

3. Beat the eggs with the vanilla essence and slowly add this to the mixture. (You can add a tablespoon of flour if the mixture starts to curdle.)

4. Stir through the milk, then gradually fold in the flour until well combined. I usually do this part by hand, but you can still use the electric mixer – be sure not to overbeat as you want your cake to be light and spongy.

5. Pour the mixture into the prepared tin, smooth over and bake in the preheated oven for 30–35 minutes or until the cake springs back when lightly pressed.

6. Allow the cake to cool in the tin completely before decorating.

7. Mix the icing sugar with cold water, the consistency should be spreadable but not too runny. Pour the icing over the cake and then cover with the sprinkles.

To make this even quicker, add all the cake ingredients
to one bowl and whisk until pale and fluffy

Add more indulgence to this childhood favourite
by serving it with custard

Harper North

would like to thank the following staff and
contributors for their involvement in making
this book a reality:

Fionnuala Barrett

Peter Borcsok

Ciara Briggs

Sarah Burke

Matthew Burne

Alan Cracknell

Jonathan de Peyer

Anna Derkacz

Tom Dunstan

Kate Elton

Sarah Emsley

Simon Gerratt

Monica Green

Natassa Hadjinicolaou

Emma Hatlen

Megan Jones

Jean-Marie Kelly

Taslima Khatun

Holly Macdonald

Rachel McCarron

Ben McConnell

Diane McConnell

Billie Michael

Alice Murphy-Pyle

Genevieve Pegg

Natasha Photiou

Sarah Prior

Florence Shepherd

Eleanor Slater

Emma Sullivan

Katrina Troy

Daisy Watt